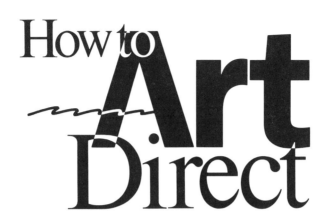

How to Art Direct

Laurence K. Withers

ISBN: 0-88108-090-X
Library of Congress Catalog Card Number: 91-0772285

First Printing 1991
Second Printing 1991
Third Printing 1996

ART DIRECTION BOOK COMPANY
456 Glenbrook Road
Glenbrook, CT 06906
(203) 353-1441 / Fax: (203) 353-1371

Table of Contents

Acknowledgments

By his very nature, the art director depends on the support and help of many other professionals – photographers, illustrators, typographers, mechanical artists, etc. It's both humbling and comforting all at the same time.

That goes for a book on art direction. There are a number of people whose help must be credited in the production of this book. Here, I'd like to humbly offer my thanks:

Don Barron realized the true potential of today's art directors far better than many art directors themselves. From the first, he saw the benefit of such a book and has encouraged me to share what I've learned about our profession.

I don't think anyone could ask for a better editor than Greg Fraser. Granted, a writer expects his editor to be the last word on grammar, sentence structure, continuity, etc. What I didn't expect was Greg's ability to guide and motivate when at times I felt the task of writing such a book was beyond me.

Cindy Yocum has been invaluable in the production and layout of the text. I also wish to mention Bruce Milley, my partner and the agency's resident computer expert. He kindly put his stamp of approval on the chapter on the graphics computer. And I can't forget Lisette Bralow whose knowledge of publishing, editing and legal issues helped to put the finishing touches to the manuscript.

I want to thank my wife, Holly, for her support, and my family for their understanding for the countless hours spent completing this work.

And finally, thanks to the Lord above for my talents are God given, and I am His steward of those gifts.

Introduction

Every year colleges and art institutes graduate thousands of graphic artists...but not one art director. There is no school that offers a curriculum in art directing. No vocational school or correspondence course exists on the subject. All art directors have to learn through a process of trial and error, on the job.

While art directors have always been taught this way, this method of learning is slow and ineffective. This book was designed to help you become a better art director – to be more efficient and knowledgeable. It was written to show you, in detail, not only what it takes to be an advertising art director, but a successful one.

In this book you'll find information concerning:

How to develop creative ideas

How to manage an art department

How to hire other artists

Estimating jobs accurately without surprise

What it takes to produce commercials

How computers will change your life

And much more

This book contains specific instruction regarding how to select models for still photography, how to negotiate with artists, the ins and outs of copyright law, learning how to brainstorm, and simple rules for presenting creative work.

Plus, you'll find many checklists, forms and contracts that art directors can use to stay on top of every situation. Such as:

Photography Checklist

Model Evaluation Checklist

Model Release Form

Production Estimate Form

Mechanical Checklist

Contracts for use when using photographers

Having been an advertising art director, and now a creative director, I've discovered what it takes to be a top art director.

The successful art director is a person with the answers; the one with the ability to create and produce effective advertising. He or she is the person who can work with, and supervise other creative team members. The successful art director is, in a word, a professional.

The purpose of this book is to set a standard of excellence for art directors. The standard has to do with detailed knowledge, sharpening creative ability and developing managerial skills. The person who possesses these characteristics will not only make a great art director, but will also have the tools to advance.

CHAPTER I

Today's Successful Art Director

"Art directors used to be the hand maiden of copywriters, but now they've gone up in the world."*

That's truer today than when David Ogilvy, one of the fathers of modern advertising, proclaimed it over a decade ago.

Previously, the art director's job was simply to execute the copywriter's ideas. The hierarchy was clear – copywriters developed the concepts and art directors produced those ideas.

Accomplished art directors could advance to senior and executive art director positions; however, it was usually the copywriter over the art director who eventually rose to creative director status.

Today this trend is changing, perhaps even reversing itself. Today's advertising is more visual. Increasingly, the concept of the ad centers around the visual or even a headline developed by an art director. Successful advertising has always depended on great concepts, but now those concepts are no longer the sole domain of the copywriter.

The art director is progressively becoming a key figure in the success of an advertising agency, taking on more

*Ogilvy On Advertising, David Ogilvy, Vintage Books, 1985

responsibility than ever before.

A successful art director must be proficient with drawing, composition, type, layout, and design. These are the basics. The art director must also be conversant with printing and print production, binding techniques, process color separation, photography, film processing, television and film production, and computer technology. But that's not all.

The art director may be likened to a building contractor who has been hired to oversee the construction of a house. The contractor coordinates the various subcontractors – carpenters, masons, plumbers, electricians, painters, and landscapers – the same way an art director manages photographers, illustrators, mechanical artists, separators, typographers, and stat houses. The art director, like the contractor is responsible for the timely completion of the work, the standard of quality, the selection of materials, and holding the line on the budget. In short, the art director should have a sound working knowledge of the various trades to ensure that each subcontracting craftsman completes his job properly.

However, unlike most building contractors, the art director is usually the architect who also designs the advertisement or commercial. Furthermore, the outstanding art director possesses skills and knowledge far beyond the realm of art, such as managerial and organizational skills, business/marketing and media knowledge, and even some writing abilities.

Ten Biggest Myths About Art Directors

This new appreciation for the art director has been hard won. It's meant overcoming many previously held myths and stereotypes regarding art directors including being:

1. **Eccentric and unpredictable**
2. **Perpetually disorganized**
3. **Deficient in copywriting ability**
4. **Without any regard for advertising budgets**

   5. Untrustworthy around clients
   6. Unconventional in dress
   7. Contemptuous of account executives
   8. Unable to follow instructions
   9. Short on presentation skills
   10. Mindless about deadlines

This book is dedicated to dispelling those obsolete and inaccurate myths.

This book is *not* about art. It has nothing to do with composition, layout, design, or how to create marker comps. This book is about what it means to be an art director; to be in charge of a department and creative people; about setting and maintaining high standards; about discipline and professionalism; and how all of this will help you get ahead.

The successful advertising art director is a vital part of the professional advertising team. He or she should be as comfortable presenting campaigns to clients as designing brochures; just as much at ease discussing marketing strategy as marking up mechanicals; as equally prepared to manage an art department as mounting ads for presentation. I believe the art director on the board today could very well be in the board room tomorrow.

There are other characteristics that make for a good art director. In addition, the following attributes are necessary:

- Maintaining meticulous work habits.

- Keeping up to date on contemporary design styles.

- Staying on top of the latest production techniques and materials.

- Developing a strong grasp of type and typefaces.

- Knowing what constitutes effective design.

- Being thorough and detail oriented.

- Demonstrating resourcefulness in problem solving.

■ Communicating ideas effectively.

■ Possessing the ability to coordinate several tasks or projects at once.

Leadership – As the job title implies it's the art director's job to direct, or lead. It may be a staff of artists or one lone photographer, but it is your responsibility to guide these people to meet your objectives. Some people are born leaders. Others of us have to develop the skills. Becoming a leader is like learning a language or playing an instrument. It means acquiring certain abilities, abilities that can be mastered. Taking a leadership role may be contrary to your artistic nature; being an artist and at the same time a leader may seem incompatible. But lead you must.

Artistic – There are art directors who cannot draw. You needn't be an artist to be an art director. You should, however, have artistic sensibilities and a knowledge of composition, color, texture, tone, perspective, etc.

Marketing oriented – The successful art director should never forget his or her real job is to sell or promote the client's services or products. Everyone enjoys seeing creative work, but it must be creative for a purpose. The greatest reward for an art director should be to help boost the client's bottom line.

Effective people skills – I heard an interview with the famous movie producer, David Brown. Mr. Brown, who is also a published writer as well as a successful producer, was asked to identify the single most important talent that helped him get ahead. His greatest talent he felt was, " Getting along with people." People are the biggest asset in any advertising agency, and it's the smart art director who gains the cooperation of the people he or she works with. It's necessary to know what motivates people, how to treat others and, perhaps most crucial, how to criticize without being destructive.

Being a team player – Advertising is a team effort. It involves the efforts of mechanical artists, photographers, separators, proof readers, traffic people, agency production people, account executives, copywriters, and many others. Learn to appreciate and lean on those other people for their opinions, knowledge and cooperation. The result will be creative advertising that's more tightly focused.

Communicating – Considering we are involved in a business concerned with communications, it's surprising more of us are not better equipped in communicating with each other. I'm referring to day to day communications with others around us as well as formal presentation of creative ideas. Effective communication is as important in advertising as it is in a person's private life.

The view of this book

Art directing is a unique profession. Where else do you have the opportunity to work on a diversity of products everyday? In what other field can you work on a television commercial one day, direct a photo session the next, and make a creative presentation to the client the next? What industry gives you such a variety of design assignments – brochures, magazines and newspaper ads, pamphlets, TV storyboards, trade show displays, etc.? What job will showcase your work in a way that it's seen by millions of businessmen and consumers?

This book is concerned with the skills and inside information every art director needs to do his or her job effectively. To that end you'll find chapters on running an art department and managing other artists. The purpose of this book is to also help you get ahead, which is why I've included two chapters dedicated to finding a job in art direction and growing beyond. You'll find more specific information about the law as it affects art directors, copyright regulations, television production, as well as an entire chapter devoted to the art director and photography. Still another chapter is devoted to art directors and computers. I believe we will be experiencing some phenomenal changes in the industry due to this new technology. Finally, I've also included a chapter entitled, **Six Things Every Art Director Should Know**; six things you may never have imagined was part of being an art director. Plus much more.

Since there's a tremendous amount of detail involved with being an art director I've included a series of checklists and forms throughout this book. Use these checklists when reviewing mechanicals, hiring models, or preparing for a photo session, to account for those things you might forget, miss or otherwise overlook. As the Bible says, "It's the little foxes that ruin the vineyards." Yes, it's the tiny details, the ones that go unnoticed which often turn into horrible catastrophes.

In essence, this entire book serves as a checklist. You'll find specific information regarding what works, what doesn't, what to look for and look out for, what to anticipate and what to expect.

Will Rogers said, "All I know is what I read in the papers." Some of what I know I've learned from reading what other people have to say. You'll notice I refer to advertising legends like David Ogilvy, William Marsteller, John Caples and others throughout this book. They have set the course for much of today's opinions regarding effective advertising.

The Philadelphia Connection. I'm writing as an art director who has spent his entire career in the Philadelphia market. You may find from your own experience that what holds true in my area may not necessarily be the common practice where you work. Terms and practices may vary but, on the whole, I believe the information in this book is universal among all advertising art directors.

If you are just starting out I know you'll find this book a real eye-opener. You'll discover things they never taught you in school. We'll talk about what professionals know but never bothered to tell anyone else. If you've been an art director for a while this book will give you the tools you need to get ahead further. And for those who have been around the block a couple of times, I hope you will find a trick or two here and there.

Refer to this book often, follow its methods, use its

checklists, and you should be on your way towards becoming the art director who succeeds.

CHAPTER II

Landing that Job

This chapter is written from two perspectives: first, as a person who's been in the job market; second, as a creative director who's hired his share of art directors. Here, we will examine what I, and other creative directors, look for in an art director.

What with mega-mergers and mass layoffs, art directors are finding the job market more highly competitive than it has ever been before. It's tough changing jobs. Tougher still for those just out of college looking for the first big break. It's the old Catch 22 – no one wants to hire someone who's inexperienced, but where do you get experience if no one will hire you? Currently the situation is so desperate that graphic artists, who have already completed their schooling are taking internships at agencies without pay, just to get their feet in the door.

Where the jobs are

Sources for finding a job include:

Newspapers – The first choice of most job hunters is probably, I must tell you, your least productive job resource. The averages are against you. For example, when my agency runs an ad for an art director, guaranteed we'll receive 150 to 175 replies. That means there's a little better than one in 150 chance you'll be called for an interview. Not as bad as playing the lottery, but there are more productive avenues.

Word-of-mouth – You've got a friend in the business? Excellent. That's a good resource for qualified job leads. Perhaps there's a position at the company where that person works. By this method you'll not only have the inside track, you'll know first-hand what the company's like and what you can expect if you are hired.

Industry organizations – Join them. That's where you'll find the movers and shakers. Get involved. Keep your ear to the ground; listen for which company just landed that big account – they might need new AD's. Let your contacts know you're looking. But be discreet if you don't want it to get back to your present employer.

Employment agencies – These agencies receive a fee for placing qualified people, which is usually a percentage of the employee's first year's salary. This fee is often paid by the employer. However, an employment service may not be for you if you're just starting out. Consider the fact that there's less money in placing an AD at $18,000 than at $36,000. Consequently, you may not receive the agency's best effort.

Industry business publications – Look in the classified sections of advertising and local business publications. Look at the Ad Notes section of those magazines – they're a good resource for qualified job leads – and note which agencies have the new accounts. Notice who was just named creative director, or the AD who's just been promoted to Executive AD, leaving a vacant art director's spot. Look for those industry people who have been interviewed in local publications and who sound like they'd be interesting to work for.

Shotgun approach – Get your hands on a directory of advertising agencies. Start at "A" and begin writing letters to the creative director at each agency and arrange an interview. This will not only help you in your current job search, but will also introduce you to who's who in your advertising community.

What's the best, most productive avenue for finding jobs? That's hard to say. You could spend years responding to the classified ads and have nothing to show for it, when out of the blue a friend will call with a hot lead that lands you in a new position.

Like baseball, it's important to cover all your bases. The success of a short stop doesn't depend solely on his natural talent, but a combination of ability, concentration, practice, advice from coaches, analyzing statistics, reviewing tapes of games, etc. I wouldn't be surprised if a rabbit's foot or two doesn't help. Each method for finding a job has a greater or lesser chance for success.

My advice is to use all the resources available to you; get all the percentages working in your favor.

Your job hunting arsenal

Before you head out into the job hunting wilderness check your gear. Do you have everything: your cover letter, resume, portfolio? Are they all in working order. Let's check and see.

The cover letter. To some employers the cover letter is an important formality, a courtesy. Responding to a classified ad and not including a cover letter is like barging into a person's office without being announced by the secretary. If you forgo the formality of a cover letter, then you'd better have an outstanding resume and samples. As an employer I think to myself, "If a person isn't savvy enough to send a cover letter, do I really want that person working for me?"

The cover letter should not merely reiterate what your

Here's a sample cover letter:

Dear Creative Director:

The average creative director spends $1557* in billable time to hire an art director. Now, I can show you how to reduce that cost significantly. I am an experienced art director with strong credentials, and I am certain that if you grant me an interview, you may very well decide that interviewing any other candidates will be unnecessary.

All I ask is one half hour of your valuable time (approximately $45 dollars in billable time). At that time I will present a brief video tape, demonstrating my skills and background, which you may keep at the end of the presentation. On this tape, I think I can show that I, as a professional art director, can benefit your company by:

■ Producing well-thought-out, creative advertising
■ Keeping tight rein on budgets
■ Coordinating work to meet all project deadlines
■ Managing successfully other artists,
   photographers, and illustrators, etc.
■ Working effectively as a team with other agency
   members
■ And more

I've also included several video references with former employers at the end of the tape.

If I have piqued your interest, I would like to arrange to play this tape and to show you a traditional portfolio of high calibre work.

Thank you for your attention and I look forward to hearing from you.

Sincerely,

Laurence K. Withers

*P.S. If you're curious as to how I arrived at the figure $1557, I have prepared a tally sheet that I will give you at our interview together.

resume says. Consider it a sales letter, like that found in a direct mail piece.

1. If you are writing to a specific individual be certain you have their correct name and title. The person will take it for granted if you do...and irritate them if you don't. If you have any doubt about the spelling of a person's name or their exact title call their company's secretary.

2. Don't wait. Get the person's attention right away. Make the opening unique by posing an interesting statement:

> Dear Executive Art Director:
> This could be the last cover letter you have to read.

Or relating an interesting fact:

> Dear Creative Director:
> There are 752 full time employed art directors in this city. Still, it's good to know there's room for talented people.

Or quoting a famous individual:

> Dear Senior Art Director:
> Please forgive the brevity of this letter, but as Willie Mays said, "I didn't come to talk, I came to hit."

You can even make it a visual grabber, such as the copywriter who sent me a pop-up cover letter showing a man behind bars. The writer pleaded to be rescued as he was being held prisoner at a recruitment advertising agency. The letter caught my attention, the fellow got the interview and subsequently the job.

3. Sell your product (yourself), state your benefits, your features, and the reason to buy (employ) you.

4. Don't tell the person what you can do. Tell that person what you can do...*for them.*

5. Keep your cover letter short, preferably to one page. There's the story of Winston Churchill who asked the Admiral of the Navy to explain on one side of a sheet of paper exactly what preparations the Navy was making in the preparedness for war.

6. Finally, tell the employer you will be calling within the next several days to follow up your letter. Be sure you do call within one or two days. If not, the CD or Executive AD may tend to forget your letter and the effect will be wasted.

The Resume. In any other profession, anything but a proper, formal resume would be inappropriate. But for the bleary-eyed creative director or executive art director who's had to wade through dozens of uninspiring letters, creativity is welcomed.

For instance, I once received a resume with a head band attached to the page headed, "I sweat to make great advertising." Then there's the young man who had his resume printed on a tee-shirt claiming "my talents and your company are a perfect fit."

At the top of most resumes you'll find the career objective or a statement of long or short term goals. Generally, these are always cliched. "I'm looking for a meaningful position that will utilize my innate talents in an encouraging environment to fully realize my true potential...so on and so on..." Avoid being too flowery. Keep it direct, but don't overdo it with, "I'm looking for more money and more vacation time."

List your meaningful education credits. College. Industry-related courses. Seminars. Personally, I don't care where you went to high school. This also applies to your experience. Don't tell me about your summer job working for McDonald's. I'd like to know about your last three jobs in advertising if you've been in the industry that long. One thing you should keep in mind; an interviewer will look to see how often you've switched jobs. Interviewing job applicants is no joy and any creative director will be reluctant to hire someone who might leave soon. If you have changed jobs frequently, you'd better be prepared with some pretty good reasons why.

Under each entry briefly outline your duties and responsibilities. List your skills under a separate heading. Can you work a stat machine? Do you have graphic computer skills? Special achievements are interesting if they're truly special. Tell me if you've won an Addy award, written a children's book, or sailed down the Amazon.

Then list your hobbies. You might find you have common ground for conversation with the person interviewing you. Any good salesman knows the longer you keep the buyer talking the greater the chance of making the sale...and getting the job. Also mention your membership in clubs and associations. For example, when someone tells me they're a member of the Philadelphia Art Directors' Club they immediately gain a point in their favor.

I prefer short resumes; one page. Also, bring extra resumes to every interview; you'll never know when an interviewer will misplace the one you sent, or you'll have to pass out copies to others at the agency.

Samples. Whet the appetite of the person receiving your cover letter and resume by including samples of your work. This will confirm your experience and give the employer a better handle in relating you to your resume.

Once I interviewed for a position with a cosmetics company only to discover they already possessed a sample of my work. It seems the company president noticed my design for an Hawaiian sweepstakes promotion for a bank. The president "borrowed" the design for her own company promotion, leaving her somewhat chagrined when I opened my portfolio.

Photocopies are acceptable if original copies of your samples are limited.

The portfolio. It doesn't matter if you went to Yale, your name is Rockefeller, or if you've been knighted by the Queen. *It don't mean a thing if it ain't got that swing.* What does matter is whether you have something to offer, and if it's evident from your book. A lot of people can talk about creativity but once the book is open "the truth be known."

The portfolio should display the full range of your

talents. For the person right out of school it should display your basic design abilities and mechanical paste-up skills. It should indicate the variety of products you've worked on, your design and layout abilities, and drawing and marker skills. But more importantly, it should demonstrate how you work and your abilities to express ideas graphically. I'm interested in seeing how you tackle a creative problem, your resourcefulness. I'm searching for a person who has ideas. I don't even mind if the ideas are somewhat impractical or wild. As Hall of Fame copywriter, John Caples put it, "You can always tame a wild idea, but a tame idea will always be tame."*

Here are some tips on how to put your book together:

1. You've heard the saying, "You only have one chance to make a first impression." Please, put your best work in the beginning of your portfolio.

2. As an art director you'll probably be working on a variety of accounts – industrial, business-to-business, and consumer – so show a variety of design projects: advertising, packaging, billboards, television storyboards, stationery and logo designs. If you know an agency is looking for a person to handle strictly food accounts, arrange your book accordingly.

3. Limit the number of samples. The person interviewing you shouldn't have to spend more than 10 to 15 minutes reviewing your book, unless they want to.

4. Arrange a minimum number of pieces on a page to avoid distracting clutter.

5. Include thumbnail sketches from one or two projects to better demonstrate how you can develop an idea.

6. If you're just beginning your job search you should ask interviewers for criticism of your portfolio – both layout and content. Don't think you're implying you lack confidence by encouraging criticism. Asking for criticism can work to your advantage in two ways: first, you'll get a better, more tightly focused book, and second, you're

*How to Make Your Advertising Make Money, John Caples, Prentice Hall, 1983

asking the interviewer to reconsider your work. That way, he or she won't forget it as easily.

7. Update continually. After a half dozen interviews you'll know which ads in your book are the winners – the ones the interviewer mulls over, compliments and interrogates you about. Then there are others that tend to get picked over more often than Charlie Brown at a Little League try out. Cut out the driftwood as quickly as you get new pieces to replace it.

What if the samples in your book don't reflect the full powers of your creativity? Then I would encourage you to create your own advertising campaigns that do. That brings to mind two occasions where artists were applying for a position with our agency. Both had portfolios comprised of completely fictional ad campaigns for real products. One fellow went so far as to have a professional copywriter write headlines and copy. I hired him.

Marketing yourself

The classified read: "Experienced art director for hire. Mint condition. Works like a dream. Resourceful, intelligent, creative. Comes with several prestigious awards. Allow two weeks to give notice and delivery. Best offer. Call after 5PM."

Absurd of course, but in a very real sense you are marketing yourself. On the one hand we have a buyer. He's the creative director, senior or executive art director, or the agency president. At some point that person is going to lay down his or her money and purchase the services of an art director at thousands of dollars a year. He or she is looking for a person with "x" qualifications, personality and experience.

Then we have *you*, the seller. You have certain abilities and talents that you feel are saleable. The only thing we need here is a meeting of the minds; an agreement that each has what the other wants and is willing to make an exchange – time and talents for money.

At first you may be uncomfortable with the prospect of

having to market yourself, but you should try to get over this feeling. Divorce yourself from the fact that it's *you* you're selling. Pretend you're selling the services of another art director and that you're his or her representative.

Tackle the situation like an interesting marketing problem. First, take stock of yourself. What exactly do you have to offer? What useful skills can you bring to the job? What artistic, marketing, and managerial talents can you promote? Be critical with your evaluation. Determine what drawbacks you have. Is it lack of knowledge regarding certain types of advertising — direct mail, food, business-to-business? Are you inexperienced in certain aspects of advertising, i.e. computer graphics, directing photo sessions, television production? Admit your shortcomings without hesitation, so that you have greater credibility when you outline your strengths. In an interview you want to emphasize your strengths and down play your weaknesses.

Once you've assessed your strengths and weaknesses, determine the size and type of agency you'd like to work for. Perhaps the big, high powered agencies suit your talents, temperament and experience. If you have less experience, you can target the smaller, low profile companies, where you can learn and build your portfolio. Research those companies that fit your criteria. Who are their clients? What are their billings? Do they specialize in TV or print? What's their reputation? Are they known as a creative shop or a sweat shop? Do they have a record of winning awards? By targeting certain agencies you have a better chance of securing a position.

Dressing for success – As with any good marketing plan you can't ignore or minimize the importance of packaging. How you dress will affect the prospective employer's perception of you. No one expects creative people to dress like IBMers, but if you want to be taken seriously you have to dress seriously.

Some of advertising's most creative figures sport traditional suits and ties. Perhaps because I own my own agency, I've become sensitive to how people perceive advertising people and especially the "creative types." I would rather be judged on the content of my ideas than the cut of my clothes.

When I hire a person, male or female, I judge his or her clothes only so far as how it fits in with our company's business-like image. I feel comfortable when people follow standard business conventions and aren't consumed with having to make a political or ideological statement by the way they dress. As William Marsteller is fond of pointing out, circus freaks are always found in the side show, never in the main tent.

The interview

Never let them see you sweat.

It could be that fish you had for dinner last night, although it's probably the knot of fear in your stomach. There you are in a strange office, covertly interviewing for another job, unsure of your qualifications, wearing a suit you just discovered has a spaghetti stain on the lapel. Why, the only thing worst could be to develop a zit.

What to do? Relax and just be yourself. If you're yourself, or a reasonable facsimile, you'll appear more relaxed. It's also true the more interviews you're on, the more you will be relaxed.

Here then is the basic scenario for your typical job interview:

The Prelude. We'll assume you're meeting with the creative director. He or she meets you in the lobby. If it's a morning interview, you may be asked if you'd like a cup of coffee. You naturally decline, in light of the six previous cups you've already had this morning. The CD then invites you to his or her office or to a conference room. You're lead through the inner sanctums of the agency. People stare as you pass by. It's natural curiosity, of course, but you can't help thinking it's the dispassionate look of those watching a pig being lead to slaughter.

Act One, Scene One. You sit. The creative director takes a minute or two to look over your resume. It's only an interview. So, why do you think you're at a police interrogation. The CD scours your resume wondering what possessed him or her to have you interview in the first place. In the meantime you look around the room. You see a number of faded awards on the wall but can't quite make out the years. It tells you something, though, when the proudly framed brochures and ads are related to coal crushing equipment. And while you're at it, the furniture looks like it's seen better days. You begin to think "they need me more than I need them." Don't get cocky.

Finished reviewing your resume, the creative director looks up with a smile. Will he level both barrels and ask, "Why should I hire you instead of my niece, who graduated from RISDY?" No. Instead he starts by asking you to, "Tell me a little about yourself."

Act One, Scene Two. *The Dance of the Seven Veils.* First, don't just regurgitate what you stated in your resume. Fill in between the lines. Talk about your last couple of jobs. Outline your responsibilities, what you learned, your accomplishments. Mention why you're interviewing presently (surely it's not merely for money).

If first impressions account for anything, then this segment of the interview counts a lot. I've heard it said an interviewer will make a decision whether or not to hire someone in the first 25 seconds of an interview. Give it your best.

Remember how you present yourself is as equally important as what you say. Again, try to stay relaxed. Be yourself, but be your *best* self. Look at the interviewer directly as you speak — look him or her in the eye. Face front, and even lean your body slightly toward the person. This shows great interest. And SMILE! That's part of good body language, too.

Don't talk too long. Two minutes is reasonable, although it may seem like a life time while you're talking.

Act One, Scene Three. Now it's the other person's turn to tell you about the position and the company. Here you may need an interpreter.

He or she starts out:

"The position is officially art director. *(What is it unofficially?)* The duties principally include layout and design, some mechanical work *(the agency has a small art department)*, and concept work. You would be the principal art person and everything that leaves the agency will bear your imprint *(lack of direct supervision. Hope you enjoy responsibility)*.

"Now I want to make this very clear *(sounds like the agency got burned before)* that this is a professional position *(get ready to sell your soul)*, and by that we mean you would be ultimately responsible for seeing that the work is done and that deadlines are met. *(Makes sense)* In other words this is not a 9 to 5 job. *(Pray you have an understanding spouse, because you won't be seeing him or her much)*. The motto we live by is 'whatever it takes.' *(Uh-o, not weekends, too)*.

"We're a young company, and so far we've done very well for ourselves. Right now we're in a growth mode *(Scrambling for new business)*. We believe this is an excellent ground-floor opportunity for the right candidate. *(Will they ask you to invest?)*. By opportunity I mean that the art director we hire now could be the senior art director of tomorrow. *(Low starting salary)*.

"We believe in promoting from within the company. We can't afford to pay like the big agencies yet *(salary confirmed)* but we are loyal to the people who stick with us. We're not so idealistic as to think you'll work here forever or that we expect you to sign an oath of loyalty *(Perhaps just a non-compete agreement)*, but we do expect our employees to be hard working and loyal in return."

The above might be typical of an interview with a small or medium sized agency. But the things a small agency expects from an art director are very likely the things desired by a larger agency – long hours, great creative, prodigious output of work, at the very least expense. Welcome to the wonderful world of advertising.

Act 2, Scene 1. *("Let's see your book")*. Everything up to this point has just been the niceties. Now it's make or break time. The cold fact is, if they don't like your portfolio, chances are you won't be hired.

To begin, give the book to the creative director. Let the person go through the book at his or her own speed. At the same time, give the CD a brief description of the work, piece by piece, stating the creative or marketing objective(s) of the piece and explain how you fulfilled the objectives. This way, a piece that the CD might have glossed over will be given due consideration. You demonstrate that you can think logically and effectively.

If you have a brochure in a sleeve, take it out and let the CD open it up to see the entire piece. Put it in his or her hands.

Don't spend undue time on any one piece, just long enough to make your point. But, if the CD seems interested in a particular piece pause to let the person dwell on it. Be prepared to answer any questions the CD might have. He or she may ask if you art directed the photo shoot, who was the photographer, who was the copywriter on the job, or how a special effect was achieved. Be prepared to answer with authority so that the interviewer believes you actually were responsible for the work and not just claiming undue credit.

If you are still employed at the agency where the work was created I would suggest not answering specific questions about the client for whom the work was created. You still have an obligation to your agency and the client. Besides, if you don't show loyalty to your present employer the interviewer will wonder what loyalty you'll give his or her agency.

What if the CD wants to keep your portfolio to review with other people at the agency? I don't think there's any point in refusing. You just have to hope they will treat your book with the utmost care. But I would suggest you set a specific time to pick it up – one or two days later, at the most.

Act 2, Scene 2. *The Home-Stretch.* You're on the last leg of the gauntlet. It's now question and answer period. The CD will want to find out more about you and you'll definitely want to find out more about the agency. But don't be surprised by any of the questions you're asked.

Bill Marsteller devised a list of questions that he would ask that, frankly, would have me squirming in my seat. For instance:

■ If you come to work here, what do you expect to be doing in five years? In 20 years?

■ What did you do last Saturday and Sunday? Take me through those days.

■ What do you most admire about your wife? (husband, tentmate)

■ In your opinion, what's the best museum in town? Why?

■ What do you think the economic situation will be a year from today?

■ If you could just get in a car and drive for 30 days, where would you go?

■ Who are your two closest friends? Tell me about them.

■ Here's paper and pencil. Take five minutes to write down the adjectives that best describe you.

■ What school would you have rather gone to than the one you did?

■ What's the greatest honor that you ever had?*

And the list goes on.

I'll be honest, I'm not as tough as Bill Marsteller with questions, but I've been on interviews that were almost as

*Creative Management, William Marsteller, NTC Business Books, 1988

probing. Be prepared.

It never hurts to ask. Now it's your opportunity to ask some questions. At the top of the list, you'll want to know about salary and benefits.

<u>Money</u>. It would be nice if all prospective employers would be forthright and tell you what the job pays. In reality, it's usually the old cat and mouse game. Be assured, the perspective employer has a figure in mind regarding what salary to pay, but the CD will be reluctant to betray the amount in case you may want less. Likewise, you're reluctant to name a figure for the same reason; the agency might be willing to pay more.

A reasonable salary for an advertising art director will vary depending on the company and the market.

Smaller agencies will offer less than the larger companies, possibly $5,000 less for the same position.

<u>Benefits</u>. The trend lately has been for agencies to do away with insurance benefits or to pay only a portion of the premium. So from your perspective, the company offering $20,000 with insurance is as generous as a company offering $22,000 without. The types of insurance provided varies from minor to major medical, long-term disability, and life insurance. Dental is rarely offered.

While you're at it, discuss the agency's policy on vacations, profit sharing, and pensions. If you feel it's appropriate at the first interview, ask about sick days and personal time.

You'll also want to know if the agency gives regular employee evaluations. The benefit of this is knowing how well you're doing, if you're living up to the agency's standards, and where you can improve. Ask how often evaluations are held and whether evaluations are tied to salary increases. At our agency we provide a two-page employee evaluation form (See Pages 59 & 60) which lists the criteria of both the general characteristics of employees and professional characteristics tailored to the specific department, such as creative, media, traffic, account executive, etc.

I've heard many art directors ask about "comp time," compensation or time off for working overtime. Generally agencies don't offer comp time. Working overtime is just the "nature of the beast" in advertising; it's what's expected. At my agency, if a person continually works overtime we try to recognize their effort by either giving them a day off or a bonus. But there is no standard policy regarding overtime work and this gift is offered at the sole discretion of the agency management.

Act 3, Final scene. As a creative director I've learned that interviews are one thing and on the job performance is another.

Ideally, I like to see the art director work on an agency assignment, to see how they work with other creatives at the agency and how he or she tackles a project. I'm sure other creative directors feel the same way. Don't be surprised if you're given a freelance assignment. Although, if an agency thinks enough of you to go this extra step they should be willing to pay for your services. Never accept a project on spec.

A good sign at this point will be if the CD introduces you to other members of the agency. You may even get a tour of the facility.

Finally, get an idea when the agency will be making it's decision.

The Epilogue. *A follow up letter is the final touch.* Don't bother with a thank you card. Instead compose a follow up letter that recaps for the CD what about you should interest him. Outline your capabilities, and how you think you could contribute to his or her agency. One typed page should be sufficient.

Getting the job you want requires two things: hard work and good luck. And if experience has taught me anything, it's that the harder you work the more good luck you'll have. Of course, it doesn't hurt to have a little patience, too. It's definitely an employer's market, and there's no shortage of talented art directors. If you're having trouble landing a job, try not to be discouraged. Even if you're highly qualified, all things being equal, many times it comes down to chemistry. You're not going to click with everyone and that goes for CD's. There is a job waiting for you out there. Just keep working and eventually you'll succeed. You're even invited to interview with me.

Chapter III

Running An Art Department:
Systems and Procedures

There will be times as an art director when you'll wish you made a living pumping gas, especially if you find yourself in charge of an art department. There are so many aspects to running a department that it's very easy to get bogged down in the details. But, I've noticed that if you take the time to establish effective systems and procedures, the details will handle themselves.

My advice to you, though – don't expect success overnight. Establishing a system you feel comfortable with may take time. While the practices set forth in this chapter have worked well at our agency, you may want to tailor them slightly to suit your own unique situation.

In this chapter we will address several major areas concerned with running an art department. These include: scheduling production; establishing a workflow system; department design; filing and storage systems; and supplies.

Learning to schedule production

In my opinion, the greatest challenge of running an art department is scheduling the production of work. While an art department is anything but an assembly line, it is concerned with manufacturing a product.

Perhaps we can take our cue from the Japanese. One reason they've emerged as manufacturing giants is their ability to plan.

That means planning for the unexpected. It means being prepared when your best designer takes sick, when creative ideas don't come quickly, when the type house loses your job, and for those times of adversity when, unexpectedly, you discover you have less than a week to create an advertising campaign from scratch. To be sure, scheduling production in an art department can be an art in itself.

Once you acknowledge the unpredictability of advertising you'll save yourself many gray hairs by learning to properly schedule the art department workload.

The production schedule board. The first thing to do: create a production schedule board, such as the one below.

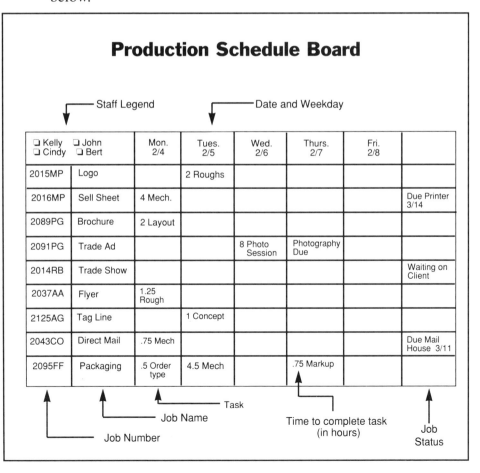

Production Schedule Board

Staff Legend							
❏ Kelly ❏ John ❏ Cindy ❏ Bert		Mon. 2/4	Tues. 2/5	Wed. 2/6	Thurs. 2/7	Fri. 2/8	
2015MP	Logo		2 Roughs				
2016MP	Sell Sheet	4 Mech.					Due Printer 3/14
2089PG	Brochure	2 Layout					
2091PG	Trade Ad			8 Photo Session	Photography Due		
2014RB	Trade Show						Waiting on Client
2037AA	Flyer	1.25 Rough					
2125AG	Tag Line		1 Concept				
2043CO	Direct Mail	.75 Mech					Due Mail House 3/11
2095FF	Packaging	.5 Order type	4.5 Mech		.75 Markup		

Staff Legend — Date and Weekday

Job Number — Job Name — Task — Time to complete task (in hours) — Job Status

Here's what to do:

1) Starting with a large chalk board or a business presentation marker board, use Letraset boarder tape and line the board as shown in the illustration on the Page 33.

2) In the far left column write the job number and in the next column the job name.

3) Along the top include the date and day of the week, with enough blocks to schedule at least a week of work.

4) Under the date headings write the task to be accomplished across from the appropriate job name. The tasks are simply written:

Layout/L/O (layout)
Rough (rough layout)
Mech (mechanical)
Markup (Mark up tissue)
Revise (Revise mechanical)
Type (order type)
Velox (order velox)
Art (order artwork)
Photo (photography session)

You may want to include other task headings such as:

Concept (concept meeting)
Appr. (client or account executive approval)
Meeting (presentation meeting with the client)

... or create your own headings

If this production board is used to coordinate production between the art and copy departments then you may also want to include these additional tasks:

Copy
Rev. Copy (revise copy)
Concept C. (concept copy)

5) In the upper left corner draw a legend where members

of the department are assigned different colors. Use this code to distinguish which members of the department are to accomplish what tasks.

You may have noticed a number preceding each task. Each number represents the number of hours estimated to complete the specific task. By assigning an estimated time for each task you should be able to avoid overloading any one artist with work. Also with a quick glance at the board you'll be able to redistribute work as needed. Under normal circumstances I would not schedule any artist for more than six hours of work in a single day. This allows for flexibility when situations like rush jobs or last minute job revisions arise, not to mention time for lunch, coffee breaks, and the normal chit-chat that's a part of any office scene.

6) Leave one last column for noting the job status, i.e. waiting on the client, when photographs are due from the photographer, when the ad closing is, when the mechanical is due at the printer.

Estimating time. In order to have a scheduling system that works effectively, it's important to estimate production time accurately. Simply "guess-timating" will never do.

So, how do you determine how long a job will take? By comparing the present job with a similar job in the past, and using the old job as a guide for the amount of time needed to complete the new job. That means keeping a strict record of time. Refer to the form on Page 36. Staple this form to the outside of every job jacket. For every quarter hour spent on a job fill in a block. And when the job is complete total the time for every task. Over a period of time you will collect a reference for estimating every type and complexity of job.

The production meeting. The sole purpose of the production meeting is to check the status of jobs in progress and to schedule new jobs. The production schedule board should be updated at this time.

The meeting should include you, members of the art

Job Time Sheet

Client   Job Name   Job#   .

Hours

Concept   ❏❏❏❏ ❏❏❏❏ ❏❏❏❏ ❏❏❏❏ ❏❏❏❏ ❏❏❏❏
           ❏❏❏❏ ❏❏❏❏ ❏❏❏❏ ❏❏❏❏ ❏❏❏❏ ❏❏❏❏   _____

Layout   ❏❏❏❏ ❏❏❏❏ ❏❏❏❏ ❏❏❏❏ ❏❏❏❏ ❏❏❏❏
           ❏❏❏❏ ❏❏❏❏ ❏❏❏❏ ❏❏❏❏ ❏❏❏❏ ❏❏❏❏
           ❏❏❏❏ ❏❏❏❏ ❏❏❏❏ ❏❏❏❏ ❏❏❏❏ ❏❏❏❏   _____

Layout   ❏❏❏❏ ❏❏❏❏ ❏❏❏❏ ❏❏❏❏ ❏❏❏❏ ❏❏❏❏   _____
Revision

Mechanical ❏❏❏❏ ❏❏❏❏ ❏❏❏❏ ❏❏❏❏ ❏❏❏❏ ❏❏❏❏
           ❏❏❏❏ ❏❏❏❏ ❏❏❏❏ ❏❏❏❏ ❏❏❏❏ ❏❏❏❏
           ❏❏❏❏ ❏❏❏❏ ❏❏❏❏ ❏❏❏❏ ❏❏❏❏ ❏❏❏❏   _____

Mechanical ❏❏❏❏ ❏❏❏❏ ❏❏❏❏ ❏❏❏❏ ❏❏❏❏ ❏❏❏❏
Revision   ❏❏❏❏ ❏❏❏❏ ❏❏❏❏ ❏❏❏❏ ❏❏❏❏ ❏❏❏❏   _____

Photo   ❏❏❏❏ ❏❏❏❏ ❏❏❏❏ ❏❏❏❏ ❏❏❏❏ ❏❏❏❏
Revision   ❏❏❏❏ ❏❏❏❏ ❏❏❏❏ ❏❏❏❏ ❏❏❏❏ ❏❏❏❏   _____

Proofing   ❏❏❏❏ ❏❏❏❏ ❏❏❏❏ ❏❏❏❏ ❏❏❏❏ ❏❏❏❏
           ❏❏❏❏ ❏❏❏❏ ❏❏❏❏ ❏❏❏❏ ❏❏❏❏ ❏❏❏❏   _____

Ordering   ❏❏❏❏ ❏❏❏❏ ❏❏❏❏ ❏❏❏❏ ❏❏❏❏ ❏❏❏❏   _____
From
Suppliers

❏ = one quarter of an hour

department and the agency traffic or production person. It's a good idea to hold a production meeting at least once a week, with a shorter meeting later in the week to introduce new jobs that have come in since the last meeting.

Production meetings typically take three times longer than they should. Attendees have a tendency to go off on tangents about creativity, the merits of one supplier over another, and a thousand and one other subjects not directly related to scheduling. The object is to spend less time at the production meeting and more time in actual production.

Here are three general rules to help ensure a successful production meeting:

1. Focus your attention on issues at hand. Save all unnecessary discussion till after the meeting. Keep all talk concise, and to the point.

2. Prepare for the meeting by reviewing the status of the jobs in production with the appropriate artist.

3. Hold meetings early in the morning or late in the afternoon to avoid unwanted interruptions. Ask the receptionist to hold all calls.

The actual scheduling is easy. If you have a job that needs to be produced in a normal turnaround time you simply begin scheduling the job at the first available date. After you assign a due date for a layout, then you know, considering the nature of the job, that two days hence you should have client approval, and five days after that photography will be due, and so on, and so on. Some tasks involved with very large projects may have to be scheduled over several days. For instance, mechanicals on a large brochure might take three days to complete.

If a job comes into the system and yet your artists are fully scheduled for the next two weeks, then you'll know you have to either

A). rearrange schedules to accommodate the new job,
B). have your artists work overtime, or
C). consider hiring freelance artists.

In the case of rush jobs you still have the same number of tasks to complete as a normal job – you just have less time. To meet production dates may mean, again, working overtime, hiring freelancers, or even paying rush charges to outside suppliers to expedite your work.

Once you have revised and posted new jobs on the board you should review the board with the other artists in your department and confirm that the new dates are realistic. It's equally important to prioritize the day's tasks for an artist. If need be, the least important tasks can be scheduled to another day if additional time is needed on a critical project. If a date cannot be met it is incumbent upon the artist to notify the art director at the earliest possible date. When a task is assigned to be completed on a certain day, it means that the artist has until the end of that day to complete the task. Make sure your account people understand that "end of the day" may very well mean 9PM.

Last words on scheduling. Keep the production board in a central location so everyone is aware of the department workload and is clear about his or her responsibility.

Maintaining a schedule takes constant supervision. Be aware that the "forces" will be working against you to undo your efforts. Listen to the words of business guru, Philip Crosby, in his book, Quality Is Free – "Good things happen when they're planned. Bad things happen on their own."*

Workflow. This refers to the flow, or orderly path of work from one person or department at the agency to the next. The flow of work in the art department should follow the chain of command as shown here:

Art Director

↓

Asst. Art Director

↓

Artist/Mechanical Artist

* Quality Is Free, Philip Crosby, Penguin, 1985

It's important that all work coming in or going out of the department should pass through the hands of the art director. The reason for this is four-fold:

1. It's the art director's responsibility to review all incoming work for clarity and completeness of instruction.

All work orders should contain a detailed description of the work to be done, the due date, printing or publication specs, sizes, line screens, whether color or black & white, etc.

2. The art director needs to schedule all work. If work is not scheduled, you can bet your bottom dollar it probably won't get done.

3. Every job should be proofed. Every job should be proofed. (*No, that is not a typo. I just wanted to emphasize the point*). Proofing is one of the most important, and most often neglected duties of the agency. Every available pair of eyes should be employed to catch mistakes. And even if your best proofreader gives his or her stamp of approval, remember the art director's artistic expertise is also crucial, so he or she should also review all boards.

Proofing shows pride in your work – that you want every detail to be right. Besides, clients don't take kindly to omitting their 800 number or misspelling the name of their product.

4. Finally, as art director you're responsible for all work that comes through your department. You'll be the one "called on the carpet" for printed mistakes. For your own peace of mind you should always review all work.

Twelve step workflow process

Here then, is a detailed workflow description:

1. The concept. Today most art directors work as a team with a copywriter in developing the concept, headline, and visual. Once you've established the creative direction, either you, the copywriter, or both, present the idea to the creative director.

2. Once the copy and concept have been approved by the CD and others associated with the account, the job comes to the art director for art production scheduling.

3. After scheduling, the art director and the assistant art director or artist review the job. (Important: Be motivational. Explain the concept fully to the artist. Inspire him or her to develop the idea, to make the piece visually exciting, and to make sure it communicates the concept clearly).

4. The next step is to have the artist create a rough layout. The art director either approves the layout – and in turn submits the layout to the creative director and the rest of the agency members who have a hand in the approval process – or returns it to the artist for modification.

5. Upon CD/agency approval, the rough layout, with or without changes comes back to the art department, to the art director and finally to the artist for final layout.

6. Once completed, the final layout goes to the art director then through the agency approval process, and is finally presented to the client.

7. If the client does not approve the layout and concept then the project goes back to the creative concept stage #1. If the layout has to be redone, make sure you have clear instructions from the AE regarding the client's objections.

When the layout and concept are finally approved by the client the project comes back to the art department and the art director for final production scheduling.

8. The art director or artist schedule photography and/or illustration, stats and typography to be done.

9. Once the photography and art have been completed and approved by the rest of the agency and the client, the job is given to the paste-up person to produce the mechanical.

10. After the mechanical is finished the assistant art

director reviews the mechanical and uses the mechanical checklist to ensure completeness. (More about the mechanical checklist below).

11. The art director, in turn, reviews the mechanical and double checks the mechanical checklist. Comparing the mechanical to the mechanical checklist is the last, and arguably, the most important procedure before any project leaves the art department. (See Mechanical Checklist, Page 42). Believe me when I say that every point covered on this list represents an actual instance which resulted in a costly mistake.

For example, number 1 reads *"note enlargement or reduction of finished piece from mechanical size"*. The particular incident involved a mechanical for a large poster which was done at 75% of the final size. Since the printer was never given the final size he printed the poster the same size as the mechanical. I strongly urge you to adopt this list or create your own. Either way, use some type of mechanical checklist.

12. The art director then releases the mechanical for agency and client review, approval, and production.

The "rush-rush" nature of advertising will always be at odds with maintaining a strict workflow procedure. To some, workflow is another word for red tape. The tendency is to want to skirt the system. Your purpose in establishing a workflow is not to create bureaucracy but, in fact, to affect the timely and accurate completion of all work, which ultimately means a well serviced, contented client.

The Physical Layout

When designing the layout of the art department, try to create an atmosphere conducive to creativity. I think all artists should have their own space, whether it's having individual offices or simply using dividers. All creative people need an area where they feel comfortable, to work in surroundings that most reflect their creative personality. There should also be an area where artists and creative people can gather for department meetings or brainstorming sessions.

Mechanical Checklist

Client_____Job Name and #_____ Date_____
Asst.

AD   AD

☐   ☐   note enlargement or reduction of finished piece from mechanical size, i.e."Final finished size Is..."

☐   ☐   check crop marks for size
☐   ☐   do photos have enough bleed
☐   ☐   does art require ruby
☐   ☐   are colors indicated on tissue
☐   ☐   are screens indicated
☐   ☐   are photo and illustration placement indicated
☐   ☐   photo and illustration linescreens indicated
☐   ☐   are drop outs indicated
☐   ☐   are position stats noted as such
☐   ☐   is live area indicated
☐   ☐   is bleed indicated
☐   ☐   is trim indicated
☐   ☐   are color chips on board ☐ coated ☐ uncoated
☐   ☐   is mech clean - all unwanted marks removed
☐   ☐   has any light, broken or cut type been corrected
☐   ☐   is all type pasted down securely
☐   ☐   check consistency - column width, type, size, boldness, etc.
☐   ☐   quality of typesetting - hyphens, letter and word spacing, etc.
☐   ☐   are all overlays registered
☐   ☐   is all type straight
☐   ☐   is the job number on the back of all boards
☐   ☐   is the stock specified
☐   ☐   is the typesetter's number on the board
☐   ☐   was the mech checked against the workorder
☐   ☐   was the mech checked against revision workorder
☐   ☐   was the mech compared with the original layout
☐   ☐   are all photos and artwork enclosed
☐   ☐   are photos and negs free of dirt or scratches
☐   ☐   check brochure/folder mechs for pagination
☐   ☐   is a mock-up of the job enclosed

Photocopies

☐   ☐   3 copies of the mech in job jacket
☐   ☐   1 copy of the entire tissue in the job jacket
_____   _____   Initials

The look and design of your art department will, of course, be dictated by the physical limitations of your space. If your art department is one room, organize it with one eye on utility and the other eye on esthetics. Consider how you can consolidate storage and filing areas, leaving the greatest room to the artists. If you have a separate space or room, devote it to storage of supplies and mechanicals, bins, stat camera, waxer, etc.

Part of the esthetics in an art department have to do with how it's maintained. Understandably, things can get a bit messy when you're scurrying to put a presentation together. But try to keep the art department, including individual offices, neat. I'm sure you can find a dozen studies that show how being concerned with neatness inhibits creativity. Pardon me, but I think that's a bunch of bunk. Cluttered space does affect a person's outlook, and a cluttered mind is only good for creating chaos.

Filing Systems

There's nothing more frustrating, short of getting your tie in the rubber cement, than not being able to find a particular job jacket or mechanical. One way to keep your blood pressure down is to establish a rigid department filing system and adhere to it religiously.

Job jackets. While a job is in progress the job jacket (which can be a folder or an envelope) should be the single source for all material relating to the job, including workorders and revision workorders, the layout and rough layout sketches, photocopies of the layout, advertising copy, photography and art work, the client's old brochures to be used as reference, etc. The job jacket should never leave the art department until the job is complete. And when a job is not being worked on, the job jacket should be filed alphabetically by client name and number in a filing cabinet. (You'd be amazed the number of minutes out of a month wasted looking for job jackets that should have been filed away). And no artist should have more than one job jacket in his or her possession at any time.

Something to consider: if the agency enters into a dispute with a client as to what was done on a job, the job jacket becomes a legal document. Therefore, all materials in the job jacket must be retained.

Bins. These are large cases made up of cubby holes, one client per cubby hole. Bins are used for storing mechanicals, in addition to layouts, larger pieces of art work, and some art supplies that can be stored vertically, such as illustration board and layout pads. You can buy heavy-duty metal shelves with dividers, or you can save money and custom build them out of wood. The most logical method for storing mechanicals is to file them by agency job number. Mark the mechanical on the back in the lower right hand corner with the job number. If there is more than one mechanical produced for a particular job, mark every subsequent mechanical with the job number and a letter: A, B, C, D, E, etc.

Before you file mechanicals, make an 8½ x 11 photo copy of each mechanical produced for the job and mark each copy with the corresponding mechanical number. Place these copies in a three ring binder in numerical order in the appropriate client divider section. This visual reference enables you to locate a mechanical if you don't know the exact job number.

Flat files. Another filing system, flat files, is a cabinet made up of wide shallow drawers where fragile materials like paper samples, finished illustrations, veloxs, contact negs, etc., are stored for safe keeping.

Plastic sleeve pages. Most photography today is shot on transparency film. These photos should be stored in plastic sleeve pages, or another photo storage system, and should be labeled with the job number and filed in sections by client.

Art supplies

Make it a practice every week or two to take inventory of the department's supplies and order those items that

Art Supply Order Form

Item		Order #	Price	Qty	Total
Krylon Crystal Clear		Qi6-1303	4.95	_____	_____
Graphics Pads	9 x 12	Q6-316-121	4.70	_____	_____
	14 x 17	Q6i-316-1542	8.95	_____	_____
	19 x 24	Q6-316-161	17.40	_____	_____
Tracing	9 x 12	Q6-240-121	2.70	_____	_____
	14 x 17	Q-240-142	5.25	_____	_____
	19 x 24	Q6-240-161	9.80	_____	_____

need replenishing. Don't end up kicking yourself for not ordering enough gray mount board the night before a big presentation.

On this page is a portion of an order form that we use at our agency. It shows the items that the art department orders most frequently. Included on the form is the distributor's product number for easy reference.

Initiating effective systems and procedures is time consuming. And like the busy shoemaker whose kids run around barefoot, we're so busy serving the needs of our clients we often don't take the time to do what's necessary to make our own jobs easier. But consider the benefits of a properly organized department: fewer mistakes, increased production, greater time saving, less anxiety, better morale, and most of all, a satisfied client. All this in mind, the only solution is to make the time.

CHAPTER IV

Managing An Art Department

According to Webster: "man" from the Latin, manus, means hand, and to manage means handling people; getting them to do what you wish with "tact and flattery."

Andrew Carnegie, the well-known steel magnate, would often boast that his employees knew infinitely more about steel and steel production than he. So what was his secret to success? He knew how to get people to do their very best. He knew how to manage people.

If you possessed no other skill than how to manage others you would be a very valuable art director, indeed. I've known marginally talented artists who were extremely effective art directors because of their exceptional managerial skills.

Managing might seem to go against the grain of an artist. Art is a very personal endeavor, but if you're going to be a successful art director, then manage you must.

You can run an art department by strict rules and regulations. However, this is not managing. Managing requires unique people skills – motivating, guiding, encouraging, being sensitive to others, and criticizing when absolutely necessary. Acquiring these skills takes years to learn and refine. Don't expect to become a virtuoso manager overnight.

How to be a successful manager

Be a leader. To be a successful manager means being a leader, and guiding artists to achieve department objectives. Undoubtedly, some are born leaders – the George Washingtons, Winston Churchills, General Pattons – but real leaders are not the ones always barking out the orders; making snap decisions. Leadership is less making the quick decision, and more making the right one. I also believe it is an ability that can be acquired.

The definition I like best comes from the advertising man, William Marsteller: "A leader is someone who has followers."* Yes, there is hope for all of us, even the Walter Mitty-est among us.

If you want to become a leader, here are my suggestions:

Be a good listener. Everyone appreciates a sympathetic ear. In general, most people are wrapped up in their own lives and experiences. They're more interested in telling you about their own problems than hearing someone else's. Learn to listen, and you will attract a following.

Contrary to popular belief, good listening is not a passive skill. Furthermore, if you listen, others just might be more willing to listen to you and your suggestions and requests.

Be consistent. Emerson said, "Consistency is the hobgoblin of little minds." I disagree. People desperately long for consistency in their lives. As a manager, your moods can and will affect others. You cannot be jubilant one moment and miserable the next. An atmosphere of inconsistency is not conducive to creativity or morale, which are critical to every successful art department. Marsteller says: "Morale is shattered by uncertainty. So if you're a son-of-a-bitch, be a son-of-a-bitch all the time."** That is extreme, but to the point.

Be positive. "Positive imaging" has become a popular catch phrase, especially in sports. You hear how the baseball player visualized his smacking a fastball over

* **Creative Management, William Marsteller, NTC Business Books.1988

the right field wall. Or how in her mind the skier saw herself negotiating every gate in a downhill slalom, gracefully, confidently. Yet the power of positive imaging is as old as the Bible. Job says, "That which I feared greatly has come to pass." Job was positive the worst would happen and it did. You'll never be an effective manager if you can't maintain a positive outlook. If you think negatively, you are doomed for failure. Furthermore, a negative perspective not only clouds your own vision, it affects others. You need to be positive and upbeat when you have a big presentation the next day. It's 1AM and all your artists' spirits have dissipated. Who's going to be the one to pull them up and on to victory? YOU!

Set a good example. *Don't do as I do, do as I say.* Do you remember your parents saying that? Well, if you didn't buy that line as a kid, what makes you think your employees are going to buy it now? Actions do speak louder than words, so listen up; a leader must set a good example. If you want others to be positive, act positively yourself. The same holds true for consistency, patience, stick-to-it-tive-ness. Your employees will follow your lead, but you have to set the standard. However you envision your art department to be you must set the standard.

Delegate responsibility. You need the help of others as much as they need yours. Don't be afraid to give your artists responsibility. It's their only way to learn and grow. Give them as much as they can handle. And don't be afraid to let them shine. Their success will ultimately cast a favorable light on you.

By the same token, when you delegate responsibility, be prepared for your employees to fail or not to live up to your expectations. Everyone makes mistakes – it's inevitable – but remember the old adage: we learn far more from our mistakes than our successes.

Stay involved. There is a tendency as leaders go up the ladder to detach themselves from the affairs of their department. I remember several scenes from the movie, Patton, starring George C. Scott, where the General visited his soldiers stationed near the front lines. They called him "old blood and guts" behind his back, but Patton knew he could depend on them to fight fearlessly in battle. How? Because his men knew that as their leader he was prepared to lead them into the fray and not just point the way. If you ever expect your troops to dig in for any pre-dawn presentation battles, you'd better be occupying the next fox hole.

Give praise. It doesn't take a psychologist to understand that everyone appreciates (and expects) praise for a job well done. When you compliment someone for good work, you're going to help increase that person's self-esteem, making it more likely that they'll do a better job in the future. Dale Carnegie stated in his book, How To Win Friends And Influence People, on the subject of leadership, "be hearty in your approbation and lavish in your praise."* He didn't mean cheap praise, either. For cheap praise is exactly that, and people will see it for what it is, a way to manipulate others.

Encouraging creativity. I'm sure you're familiar with Japanese bonsai, delicate miniature trees. These perfectly proportioned dwarfs are grown by cutting off the tap roots that normally allow a tree to grow to full size.

The California redwood grows unhampered, reaching a height of over 300 feet. Yet, at one time the bonsai and the redwood were the same size. Both started out as seeds weighing less than a tiny fraction of an ounce.

Creative people are like seeds. You can feed them on compliments and recognition, and watch their confidence and ability flourish. Or you can stymie their growth with negative criticism, negative feedback, even by just withholding warranted praise.

Animal trainers have long employed successfully the technique of praising and rewarding animals whenever they show the slightest improvement. Yet, most people are reluctant to give praise, fearing that while building an associate up, they are simultaneously knocking themselves down. But the person who is free to compliment others will always attract a following. Remember the adage: you can't

*How To Win Friends And Influence People, Dale Carnegie, Pocket Books, 1981

row a person across the river without going there yourself.

I'm not suggesting that you hand out meaningless compliments. That would be counter productive. Marsteller would say, that "praise makes a good person better, and a bad person worse."* The idea is to be ready to compliment when it's deserved.

Suppose some of your people don't merit praise. Impossible. Andrew Carnegie had this philosophy: It takes processing tons of ore to extract one ounce of gold. The secret to successfully mining the substance is not to look for the ore, but to look for the gold. That's it – look for the gold in others.

Set the standard. Air Force recruitment ads say it in just two words: Aim High. Everyone can appreciate the monetary awards that come with success, but for creative people, (all people, for that matter) the driving force to work is to achieve; not just to do your best, but to be the best.

Who or what is the best is debatable. How to get to be the best is not. It takes hard work and determination to rise to the top. But first you must establish goals.

As manager, you set the goals for others; for your department. The goals may vary. One goal for certain would be to encourage and produce creative advertising – not just creativity for it's own sake, but creativity for the purpose of selling the product. Consider the motto of Benton & Bowles: *If it doesn't sell, it isn't creative.*

In 1955 David Ogilvy was on his way to his first shoot for new client, Hathaway Shirts. Recently he had read that photos with "story appeal" attract significantly more reader attention. Rather than settle for your standard fashion shot, Ogilvy wrote down various ideas for giving his photo illustration story appeal. One was to have the model wear an eye patch he picked up on the way to the photographer's studio. It cost just 59¢, but the result was one of the most successful, memorable campaigns in advertising. Creativity for the product's sake.

*Creative Management, William Marsteller, NTC Business Books, 1988

Another goal is to achieve and maintain the highest standards of quality. If you want unique advertising, if you expect all work to be well thought out and meticulously executed, if you want the agency's work to reflect contemporary design, if you want it to be hard-hitting, persuasive, then think, it all has to start with *you*. You must let others know what you expect from them and then you must be relentless about achieving it.

The other side of the coin, the way to higher standards is to reject all work that doesn't meet those standards. This is more difficult than you think. It's dangerously easy to fall into the trap of accepting less than perfect work. It's tempting to "let it slide." You can rationalize all you want; how you can't stay to finish the job properly because the softball team is counting on you tonight, or the club members expect you to make the meeting; and after all the client isn't very discriminating and will never notice the ad wasn't done right; besides in 2000 years who's going to know the difference anyway...and so it goes. Once you let one thing slide then it's easy to let something else slide. Before long you're caught in an avalanche of mediocrity and botched jobs.

It is emotionally difficult to confront artists when you know their work is not acceptable, but if you don't let your people know your expectations then don't be surprised when their work doesn't meet those expectations.

The climate for creativity

Under what conditions do creative people create? For some it's a few throw-pillows and some incense. For Michelangelo it was painting the Sistine Chapel on a scaffold forty feet in the air.

David Ogilvy says he would meet briefly with "John Barleycorn" in the evening before he would sit down to write advertising copy. An agency person I know keeps a pad and pencil in his bathroom where he says he does some of his best thinking (and reading). And a creative director I worked with said his finest ideas came at four in the morning, waking him from a deep sleep and leaving him in a cold sweat.

Question. Are there any specific ways to create an atmosphere of creativity?

Perhaps. For instance, I feel people need to be comfortable with their surroundings. I'm not talking about Lazy-Boys in the art department. By comfortable I mean a person has to feel at ease. Feeling at ease could be playing rock music on the radio. Maybe it's dressing casually. It could be comfortable furniture. And I wouldn't discount an occasional round of nerf basketball to put people in an elevated mood to create.

In the final analysis, though, creativity comes from creative people. If you want high calibre creative work you must first hire highly creative people. You cannot take a basically non-creative person and teach them to be creative. In the same way, you cannot prevent a creative person from being creative. Truly creative people are compelled to create – anywhere, anytime, and often under adverse conditions.

Hiring

In Chapter 2, we discussed landing a job as an art director. In this chapter the shoe is on the other foot. Someday, if not already, you will have to interview and hire artists and art directors.

The quality of the agency's work depends upon selecting the best people. Not only talented, experienced individuals, but personalities who'll mix well with your present employees.

Hire cautiously. With equal regard for the hiree. Be careful to avoid luring someone from their current position only to discover that the person is not the art director you thought he or she would be.

Hire the best. Even if that means better than you. David Ogilvy would give the new head of every Ogilvy & Mather office a gift with the inscription: *If each of us hires people who are smaller than we are, we shall become a company of dwarfs. But if each of us hires people who are bigger than we are, we shall become a company of giants.*

Where to look for talent. In hiring artists it's a matter of supply side economics. There are hundreds of artists at any one time pursing jobs in advertising graphic design. Even so, finding the most talented at the right salary is often a Herculean task.

There are several avenues for discovering the ideal candidate:

Classified ads. On the plus side, running an ad in the classified pages might net you hundreds of inquiries. On the down side, you will have to review all those resumes. If you receive 150 letters, 144 will be either over-qualified, under-qualified, live too far away, have an erratic job history, demand too much money, have limited skills, etc. If you get six possible candidates, you're doing pretty well. After all, you only need one person to fill the position. Let me offer two bits of advice: (1) advertise only in the Sunday edition for the greatest readership and response, and (2) do not list your company's name or phone number. You will avoid a deluge of phone calls. Instead, have all responses sent to a post office box.

The "old boy (or girl) network." Use your friends and business acquaintances as resources. But avoid hiring relatives or friends; it's a sure way of spoiling a valuable relationship.

Employment agencies. They're costly, but they can save time. Some specialize in advertising personnel.

Art directors clubs or graphic arts associations. Every major city has at least one. Being a member of the Art Directors' Club of Philadelphia has helped me. The club is a gold mine of talented people.

One other excellent method. To track down talent call the placement office at area art schools and colleges. Make it a point to attend student portfolio reviews. If you're looking for an entry level staff member, you may meet that diamond in the rough. (Besides, if you want to put your finger on the pulse of graphic design in your area, check with the young talent at these schools. You'll see a lot of great ideas).

Interviewing. After narrowing the field of prospective job candidates interviewing begins. This is a nerve racking process, for both the interviewer and the interviewee. Try to establish a relaxed atmosphere. You want the interview to be a meaningful dialogue, not just an advanced game of "20 questions." Start off with general questions. Ask the candidate to take you through his or her typical work day. Ask about his or her special interests.

Take note of how the person is dressed. Ask yourself if you think they fit in to the image of the agency.

The interview is also for the benefit of the job candidate. You want the prospect to be as sure about working for the agency as you want to be about him or her. Sell the candidate on the prospect of working for you. Tell the candidate about the agency's history, it's work ethics and creative philosophy. Describe the job in detail. You may want to give them a written job description if that's available. On Page 55 you'll find a job description we use at our agency. I've occasionally given applicants a copy of our employee handbook.

Finally, you'll want to review their portfolio. This will naturally represent their best work so don't become enamored too quickly. Ask plenty of questions: *What was the objective of this ad? Did you work with the copywriter on this concept? Who was the photographer? How did you achieve this effect?* Note if the job candidate has included layouts demonstrating their marker skills. Ask to see sketches and thumbnails. This should indicate their creative problem-solving skills and the ability to convey an idea through design. Ask the interviewee which is his/her favorite ad. Their most effective ad? They may not be one and the same.

The key to hiring is to be cautious and thorough. Once you feel you have the ideal candidate do the following:

1. Tell the prospective employee you'd like to have them do one or two freelance projects for the agency. If they are unemployed or working freelance have them in for several days to work with others in the department.

Art Director
Job Description

The person holding this position reports to the senior art director and is responsible for the following:

- Follow guidelines established for the creative department
- Work with other creative department members in developing ideas for advertising and communications materials
- Developing layouts, mechanicals, and storyboards for advertising, print collateral and broadcast productions
- Assist in new business activities
- Assist in new business presentations
- Manage the working schedules of junior and freelance artists
- Review layouts and mechanical deadlines, working overtime when necessary to meet those deadlines
- Meet with clients when necessary
- Produce television commercials
- Select talent/models for print or television advertising
- Manage his or her time and prioritize assignments
- Develop production cost estimates
- Update creative department forms and checklists when necessary
- Work within established budgets when specified
- Make creative presentations to clients when necessary
- Behave and present him or herself outside the agency in a manner keeping with the agency's image
- Help maintain job jackets and other job related paperwork
- Learn to use typesetting and computer equipment and assist with typesetting when needed
- Maintain type and stat equipment
- Order, stock, and maintain supply of art materials

2. Don't hire the person without having them interview with at least two other people in your agency.

3. Check references. Ask former employers about the applicants performance, work habits, temperament, and ability to work and get along with others. Ask specific questions – not "Is Tom a nice person?" or "What was your opinion of Jane's work?" Rather, ask probing questions such as, "how does Tom respond in stressful situations?" or "how does Jane react to criticism?"

4. Refrain from hiring anyone on the spot. Give it a couple of days to let your enthusiasm cool. Step back and consider the person more critically.

After you've filled the position, write the other candidates informing them of your decision. If the choice was not easy, say so and tell them you appreciate their time to meet with you, and that you will keep their resume on file. After all, the person you hire may not work out.

Don't stop interviewing prospects just because you don't have a position to fill at the present time. When artists call to show their books take the time to see them. Maintain a list of eligible artists now so when an artist leaves you won't get stuck having to fill a position at the last minute.

Firing. If it were a matter of someone stealing art supplies from the company or insulting the clients, firing would be a mundane task. If you've given the person the chance to improve their performance, but still the situation doesn't improve then it's time to bite the bullet and let them go. Don't wait. Let them go immediately. You're displeasure will be apparent, and the morale of your department will suffer.

I would caution you to protect yourself and the agency. Even before you make your final decision, document the person's actions and conduct in detail on a daily basis and be specific about dates. Document any meeting with the person when discussing the problem. You certainly want to avoid any legal suits against the agency for an unfair firing.

Employee Evaluations

Every employee should get a complete evaluation once a year. Evaluations are not only important to help employees maintain a standard of excellence, they offer employees greater peace of mind knowing where they stand with the company regarding their work and level of performance.

Included in this chapter are sample employee evaluation forms. They're not used only to critique an artist's or art director's artistic and creative progress, but also general characteristics that you would expect of any employee, regardless of the department. Review these forms before the actual evaluation meeting. Don't breeze through them. Consider each point thoroughly in regard to the evaluee. Don't give unduly high scores out of charity, otherwise the evaluee will think they have no room for improvement in a particular area. You'll also simplify matters if between evaluations you keep a diary highlighting the employee's achievements, noting work habits, and any disciplinary needs.

The evaluation meeting with the employee should be candid, relaxed, and up-beat. Never make it a "chewing-out" session. The aim is to maintain and improve performance. Consider it as an employee tune up. Always keep in mind that you want to urge the employee on to better, more creative work. Discuss how the evaluation system works and how you went about arriving at the different scores.

Go over these evaluation forms point by point. Look for areas in which to compliment the employee. At the same time be honest about those areas where the person could use improvement, and suggest ways to help. Be prepared to give examples if you're asked to be more specific. Be open and encourage discussion. Don't be afraid to change a score if the employee convinces you a low score is not warranted.

The evaluation meeting might last one to two hours. At the end, request that the evaluation be signed if the evaluee is in agreement. Then make the evaluation a part of the employee's permanent record.

It wouldn't be a bad idea to get an evaluation yourself periodically from your creative director or executive art director. No one is above improvement.

Raises, Bonuses and Promotions

As an art director you may not have direct control over the amount of somebody's raise, but your opinions are valuable and should be sought by the agency management. Salary raises are usually tied to the employee evaluation and generally given on the eve of the employee's date of hire. While the evaluation plays a large part in determining the amount of the raise, other determining factors are: cost of living adjustments, going rate for a person with comparable talents, length of employment, etc.

Employees should be asked not to divulge the size of their raise. Or even their base salary. Our agency lost a valued employee when a talkative bookkeeper let it be known someone else was being paid more money.

Occasionally you'll have an employee whose work, or general performance goes well beyond the call of duty. In addition to a salary increase, you may also want to give them a bonus.

Some agencies give out promotions and titles the way a gum ball machine dispenses gum. It seems at some of the larger agencies, everyone is a vice president. Recommend promotions when warranted; when the artist has gained the experience and ability to handle the added responsibility of a higher position.

How to criticize

I don't have to tell you how sensitive this subject is. Be particularly careful when criticizing. Always be aware that your purpose in criticizing is to help others, to make them better artists and art directors.

As ridiculous as it may sound, I still remember Mary Poppin's advice, "Just a spoonful of sugar helps the medicine go down." If you have to criticize, start by telling

❊❊ Confidential ❊❊

Employee Evaluation

General Characteristics

Employee Name _____ Date _____

Scale: 1=not evaluated 2=unsatisfactory 5 average 10=outstanding

Characteristic	*Rating*
A. Judgement	1 2 3 4 5 6 7 8 9 10
B. Productivity	1 2 3 4 5 6 7 8 9 10
C. Self-Starter	1 2 3 4 5 6 7 8 9 10
D. Organization	1 2 3 4 5 6 7 8 9 10
E. Attention to detail	1 2 3 4 5 6 7 8 9 10
F. Thoroughness	1 2 3 4 5 6 7 8 9 10
G. Motivation	1 2 3 4 5 6 7 8 9 10
H. Leadership	1 2 3 4 5 6 7 8 9 10
I. Cooperation	1 2 3 4 5 6 7 8 9 10
J. Attitude toward job	1 2 3 4 5 6 7 8 9 10
K. Loyalty to agency	1 2 3 4 5 6 7 8 9 10
L. Appearance	1 2 3 4 5 6 7 8 9 10
M. Punctuality	1 2 3 4 5 6 7 8 9 10
N. Attendance	1 2 3 4 5 6 7 8 9 10
O. Accepts responsibility	1 2 3 4 5 6 7 8 9 10
P. Applies ability	1 2 3 4 5 6 7 8 9 10
Q. Adapts to change	1 2 3 4 5 6 7 8 9 10
R. Decisiveness	1 2 3 4 5 6 7 8 9 10
S. Stability	1 2 3 4 5 6 7 8 9 10
T. Potential for advancement	1 2 3 4 5 6 7 8 9 10

If outstanding potential for advancement is rated, indicate the next step recommended._____

_____

_____

As supervisor, what are you doing to train this employee? _____

_____

❋❋ Confidential ❋❋
Employee evaluation

Art Department/Professional Characteristics

Employee Name _____ Date _____

Scale: 1=not evaluated 2=unsatisfactory 5=average 10=outstanding

Characteristic	*Rating*
A. Basic graphic skills	1 2 3 4 5 6 7 8 9 10
B. Creativity	1 2 3 4 5 6 7 8 9 10
C. Originality	1 2 3 4 5 6 7 8 9 10
D. Sound knowledge of client business and market	1 2 3 4 5 6 7 8 9 10
E. Versatility of style	1 2 3 4 5 6 7 8 9 10
F. Resourcefulness (ability to generate several approaches to a creative problem)	1 2 3 4 5 6 7 8 9 10
H. Good taste	1 2 3 4 5 6 7 8 9 10
I. Ability to communicate ideas	1 2 3 4 5 6 7 8 9 10
J. Oral presentation skills	1 2 3 4 5 6 7 8 9 10
K. Awareness and management of costs – both the client's and the agency's	1 2 3 4 5 6 7 8 9 10
L. Estimating ability	1 2 3 4 5 6 7 8 9 10
M. On target with objectives and strategies	1 2 3 4 5 6 7 8 9 10
N. Meets deadlines	1 2 3 4 5 6 7 8 9 10
O. Broadcast production abilities	1 2 3 4 5 6 7 8 9 10
P. Advertising knowledge	1 2 3 4 5 6 7 8 9 10
Q. Marketing knowledge	1 2 3 4 5 6 7 8 9 10
R. Rapport with clients	1 2 3 4 5 6 7 8 9 10
S. Effectiveness in preventing or mitigating write-off cost	1 2 3 4 5 6 7 8 9 10
T. Interaction with other creative members	1 2 3 4 5 6 7 8 9 10
U. Fulfills written job description	1 2 3 4 5 6 7 8 9 10
V. Other _____	

the person something you admire about them or their work. In this way you might help the person accept criticism much more easily.

Personally, if I have to criticize I wait until a time when the person's co-workers are not around. David Ogilvy recommends not calling the person into your office, rather, go to them. It's less threatening. The Japanese go even further. They avoid *all* confrontation in the work place. If they need to address a problem with an employee they arrange a meeting outside the office, for lunch, perhaps.

Criticism is also less anxiety producing if you can offer concrete suggestions as to how to avoid a problem in the future. And let the person know you have confidence in their ability and that the mistake is easily corrected.

Art and Politics

Want to know the best way to destroy the peace and tranquility of your department? Allow politics. An art department is no place for employee politics. I know. In my career I've been consumed with such matters as to how many square feet my office has over one of my peers, and trying to guess if the AD next door was making more money, and jockeying to get the next promotion. The effect of politics is low morale, distrustfulness, and uncooperativeness. Hardly the atmosphere in which to produce great advertising.

Politicians in the ranks aren't hard to spot. They're the ones who flatter their superiors, while abusing those below them. They will disparage their co-workers, while glorifying themselves. They will go so far as to tell boldface lies.

I feel politics start at the top. If you allow it to happen, it will. Once you see a problem, nip it in the bud. Route it out by the roots, if you have to. Let everyone who works for you know that the way to get ahead is hard work, intelligence and honest effort. If a person you suspect of playing politics makes an accusation regarding another employee, ask the other person to come into your office and let the politician make his or her accusations face to face.

Essential reading. Managers are the fastest growing segment of the work force. If you're interested, you can find hundreds of books on how to manage. To me the best is <u>How to Win Friends and Influence People</u>, by Dale Carnegie. Although written over 50 years ago, the simple truths about people and how to get along with others are still absolutely on target. His course for businessmen is still widely attended.

Managing others can be disconcerting. But once you start to master the skills involved, you'll not only find them beneficial in the workplace, but in your everyday life as well.

CHAPTER V

6 Things Every Art Director Should Know

Today's successful art director is really something of a renaissance person. To be effective he or she has to be well versed in many areas other than art. The topics discussed in this chapter may not fit into your everyday job description of an art director, but they will come in handy if you're trying to get ahead.

1. How to make a creative presentation

In a survey, people were asked to rate their greatest fears. Number two on the list was fear of dying. What was number one? Fear of speaking in public. People would rather die than speak face to face before others! You will gain respect and go further if you master the skills involved in making a quality presentation.

There is a book I own entitled, <u>Speakers Are Leaders.</u> In the title alone there's great truth. When a person gets up to speak he's often there to persuade, seek a decision, or call others to action. Good public speakers are not timid souls. They're not without an opinion. They're not without a direction.

Making a creative presentation is one form of public speaking. Your objective in presenting the agency's creative work (ad layout, storyboards, etc.) will be to persuade the client that your executions are some of the best ways to meet his or her company's marketing goals. You are convincing the client that his or her marketing objectives are being met by your advertising concepts.

There are many details involved with making a formal presentation, and as many books on the subject. But let me give you my basic recipe for making a successful creative presentation.

1. Be prepared. This is the single greatest factor in making a successful presentation. There's no substitute for knowing your subject. And don't just know it, know it intimately! Be prepared to tell how the idea was conceived; how it meets the specific objectives; how it can be produced reasonably within budget. Lacking any formal speaking skills, just being properly prepared will probably get you through the presentation. Try to be as well acquainted with the presentation material as you are with yourself. For instance, if I were to ask you a question about yourself, you being an authority on yourself would probably answer me directly and without hesitation. That is ideally how well you should be acquainted with the creative work when making a presentation.

2. Present by objectives. You'll have a greater chance of having your work approved by the client if early in your presentation you state the advertising objectives. Start out by saying something like, "The purpose of this commercial is to re-enforce the product's marketing position, which is that Charmin' bathroom tissue is incredibly, squeezably soft." Or, "The objective of this ad is to promote Acme Stores double-coupon promotion."

3. Show only one ad or commercial at a time. Don't reveal all your work at one time. Every ad deserves special attention. If the client sees work before it's formally presented he/she may begin forming opinions prior to explanation of the work. If the client misinterprets your idea, you may not be convincing and a good idea will be lost forever.

4. Describe the ad before you show it to the

client. Like most lasting relationships it's important to take it slow. Don't just go bang, "here it is." Get the client comfortable with what he or she is going to see. Begin by describing the essential details of the main visual, without actually showing the layout. Don't mention anything about headline or concept. (Secret: If you find it difficult to remember all the details of the layout, write a description, or paste a reduced copy of the ad to the back of the board).

After you've finished describing the ad, turn the board around and read the headline and subhead aloud. Briefly describe why you think the ad works, meets objectives, and what you anticipate the consumer reaction will be.

5. Hand the ad to the client. There is a tried-and-true sales method that says once you put the product in the buyers' hands they begin to see it as theirs. Let the client explore the ad for themselves and get involved in the work. Encourage questions and discussion. This will generate greater interest in your presentation.

Here are more general aspects of presentation that you should keep in mind.

Capture audience interest. At the beginning of your presentation it's always good to gain the audience's attention through some sort of device, whether it's a visual hook, a humorous story or anecdote, or a compelling question. Whatever attention grabber it is, it should relate to the concepts you're presenting. For instance, igniting a dollar bill to emphasize that the wrong creative appeal in your advertising is like burning money.

Dress appropriately. A formal presentation requires dressing correctly, even if you know the client will be dressed more informally. Dressing properly tells the client that you take your assignment seriously. It doesn't have to be blue pin-stripped suits; remember you're still a creative person and, believe it or not, clients may expect you to dress a little more freely. But, dress in coordination with the other agency representatives.

Dealing with stage fright. A degree of nervousness can be a good thing. The trick is to be able to channel that nervous energy into making a more dynamic presentation. Problems arise when nervousness becomes paralyzing and inhibits your effectiveness. People have used different methods over the years to deal with this situation. Some people like to visualize the audience naked. Seriously. They feel that by seeing the audience without clothes puts them at a psychological advantage.

On one particular opening night the great opera tenor, Caruso, was overcome with stage fright. He was heard talking to himself in the wings, "Out! You miserable 'little me,' get out of my way! Out! Out!" He felt that he could exorcise his own demons of self-doubt this way.

A method I like is reminding myself that I am there to help the client and to help the client's business grow. I develop a positive, almost "good Samaritan" image about myself. I say to myself, "How could the client find fault with what I'm saying if the spirit of what I'm presenting is intended to benefit his or her company?

You should remember this – the audience/client wants you to succeed. They don't want you to make a bad presentation any more than they want to sit through one. They want you to present the greatest work ever conceived. Clients expect that you are the expert and unless shown otherwise they'll be on your side.

Practice makes perfect presentations. Get comfortable presenting your work. Go through several trial runs by yourself and then in front of other agency members. Video taping your presentation will also show you ways to improve.

Take note of your posture and mannerisms. Are you standing straight or slouching? Do you tend to fidget? Are you maintaining eye contact with those in the room?

Consider those characteristics you find disturbing about your presentation style and attempt to correct them.

KIS. Keep it simple. There's a story that goes that President Calvin Coolidge, upon returning from church, was asked by his wife as to the subject of the pastor's sermon. Calvin's reply, "Sin." His wife wanted to know what he had to say regarding sin. Calvin: "He was against it."

Make your main points clear, simple and concise. Don't be long-winded. Don't oversell your ideas. If they're good ideas they won't need much selling. Give the client just enough information on which to make a decision.

You would do well to follow President Franklin Roosevelt's advice, "Be direct, be brief, be seated."

2. What is a marketing plan?

Have you ever read a marketing plan? They're readily available from your account executives. You say you don't even understand what marketing is? Well, here now is your own crash course in marketing.

Marketing, simply put, is the study of how different products and services are sold. This involves the various factors of pricing, product name, channels of distribution, market research, product positioning, competition analysis, marketing strategy, and, oh yes, advertising.

Advertising, for which the art director and copywriter are responsible, is just one part of the "marketing mix." It makes sense: The better you understand marketing, the more effective will be the advertising you create. A good place to start your study of marketing might be an advertising marketing plan.

A marketing plan can run several pages or several hundred. The length will depend on the size of the company and the complexity of its needs. Either way, most marketing plans will have certain elements:

Situation analysis. This section of the marketing plan is a brief overview of the client's business, examining trends and situations, and attempts to place the client in the market relative to the competition.

> "...With the great advances in manufacturing technology, the widget market has become highly competitive. Our client, Widgets International, is a US based firm currently selling low cost, quality widgets in an assortment of fluorescent colors..."

Marketing objectives.
This portion outlines the specific goals of the marketing plan. No, "making more money" is not a valid marketing objective. Marketing objectives should be more specific than this.

Objective 1: To increase name recognition of International Widgets
Objective 2: To secure new distributors for the client's products
Objective 3: To broaden the consumer base

Marketing Strategies.
Once you've established your objectives you must determine how you will accomplish them

Strategy: Increase awareness of the client's product through a series of print advertising campaigns and direct mail efforts.
Strategy: Recruit new distributors through a direct mail solicitation campaign and trade magazine advertising.
Strategy: Develop a sales presentation designed to demonstrate the benefits of using International Widgets, to current widget users and prospective widget consumers.

Problems and Opportunities.
Often there are situations not directly related to the marketing objectives but which must still be addressed before your marketing plan is complete.

> **Problem:** American Widget, is running a vicious advertising campaign against our client's product, claiming it lacks standards of quality in its manufacturing process.
> **Opportunity:** Create a mail campaign to qualified, heavy widget users which states that International Widget will fly any buyer of widgets, all expenses paid, to their modern manufacturing facility in Tripsen Falls, KA, to see for themselves the standards of quality that goes into manufacturing an International Widgets' widget.

In addition, a thorough marketing plan will discuss the topics of:

Media placement – including a schedule of where, when, and how often the advertising will run

Competitive analysis – which focuses on the various aspects of the competition's own advertising efforts

Audience profile – a demographic and psychological study of target consumer group(s)

Positioning statement – Based on research, the positioning statement is an indication as to where the client's product stands in the mind of the consumer. Take this position statement, for instance:

> *Among soft drinks 7Up is a refreshing alternative to darker, more robust cola drinks.* From that positioning statement the creative department developed the positioning line: *7Up. The Uncola.*

Creative Strategies – Just as the marketing objectives and strategies give direction to the larger marketing plan, the creative strategies direct or act as guidelines in producing advertising creative work. Ask yourself, should the approach be humorous? Would a talking head prove most effective? Should the ad be copy intensive? Would black & white be more suitable than color? These questions will help you formulate your creative strategy.

Your study of marketing will give you a greater appreciation of the different disciplines involved in taking a product to market. Once you begin to see yourself as part of the marketing mix the more effective will be the advertising you produce.

3. How to produce ideas

As an art director you're probably intuitively creative. However, we've all had those occasions when we've been stumped by a creative project. If we had to wait until the light of inspiration hit us before laying pencil to paper, we'd all be doing a whole lot of waiting and very little advertising.

Creativity is not magic. It's a skill – a skill that once acquired needs constant practice. If we can identify the principles and methods of creative thinking then we can expedite the creative process. In his little gem of a book, <u>A Technique for Producing Ideas,</u> advertising man James Webb Young concludes, "...that the production of ideas is just as definite a process as the production of Fords; that the production of ideas, too, runs on an assembly line; that in this production the mind follows an operative technique which can be learned and controlled."*

Young outlined a five step method for producing and developing ideas, based on his own experience as an advertising creative director; and scientists and psychologists have confirmed his conclusions regarding the creative process.

This is the Five Part Method:

1. The first step is to gather existing data. That may seem obvious – you have to know something about the product before you can create advertising for it. Yet, you'd be surprised how many art directors and other creatives jump head first into a project without finding out everything they need to know. Review old brochures, study trade literature, talk to the client and visit the manufacturing facilities. Talk to the men and women on the assembly line, the sales reps, and the consumer. Use the product or service for yourself. Hunt out information wherever you can, like a bear sniffs out honey.

2. The next step is to mentally digest the bits of information you've acquired. This stage is more difficult to describe because there's no set formula. It involves reexamining the data, analyzing various facets of the project, drawing associations, and otherwise letting everything you've learned marinate in your brain. Young describes it this way, "What you do is to take the different bits of

---

*A Technique for Producing Ideas, James Webb Young, NTC Business Books, 1988

material which you have gathered and feel them over, as it were, with the tentacles of the mind. You take one fact, turn it this way and that, look at it in different lights, and feel for the meaning of it. What you are seeking now is the relationship, a synthesis where everything will come together in a neat combination like a jig-saw puzzle."* During stage two vague and partial ideas will come to you. Jot them down. These might be the beginnings of a solution.

Young warns, there will also come a point in this stage where your mind will tire of the process. Marathon runners call it "the wall", where they feel like they can't go on any further. Don't give up; you're bound to get your second wind. Climb the wall.

3. Eventually, though, you will reach a point of hopelessness, where everything seems like a jumble. This is a sign you're ready for stage three.

If you've ever read Sherlock Holmes you'll know it's not unusual that in the middle of a tough case, the famous sleuth will abandon the chase and go off to see a concert, or suddenly start playing his violin for hours – all to the great consternation of his partner, Dr. Watson. No doubt, Holmes' creator, Arthur Conan Doyle, was familiar with the creative process, for this strange behavior on the part of the detective represents the third stage of the creative process.

Stage three is a matter of turning the problem over to the creative unconscious, the intuitive parts of your brain. I'm sure you've heard someone wrestling with a tough decision say, " Let me sleep on it."

Young compares the various stages of creating ideas to the body's digestive system. "In the first stage you have gathered your food. On the second you have masticated it well. Now, [in stage three] the digestive process is on. Let it alone – but stimulate the flow of gastric juices."

4. EUREKA! If you've successfully accomplished

*A Technique for Producing Ideas, James Webb Young, NTC Business Books, 1988

stages 1 thru 3 then "you will almost surely experience the fourth." That is, the idea will appear. It will be when you least expect it – while you're shaving, or bathing, or driving to and from work – normally during a period of rest and relaxation when you aren't straining for the answer.

5. Once you've gotten over the euphoria of the fourth stage you will then enter the final stage. This last stage entails exposing the idea to what Young calls "the cold, grey dawn of the morning after."* You've planted and nurtured this idea, and it's just begun to sprout. But will it survive? Will it stand up to objective cross examination? You have to ask yourself, does it fulfill the objectives? Is it an idea upon which you can expand and build a campaign? Is it inspiring to others? Ask those who aren't as close to the idea to examine it for themselves. If it's truly a good idea they may be able to draw on your original idea and add new perspectives, to strengthen it.

This five step method is deceptively simple. It is not beyond the capabilities of most creative people but it does require practice and considerable concentration.

4. How to brainstorm

Brainstorming is a process many creative advertising people employ to generate many ideas quickly. Briefly stated, brainstorming is group thinking, where a number of people from the creative team, art directors and copywriters, pool their mental resources to solve a creative problem.

The concept of brainstorming is not new. It was first popularized by Alex Osborn, the "O" in BBDO, in his 1948 book, <u>Your Creative Power</u>. This technique has since been used effectively by government agencies, universities, think tanks, and industry.

Osborn formulated a set of rules for successful brainstorming meetings that are still used today.

---

*A Technique for Producing Ideas, James Webb Young, NTC Business Books, 1988

Osborn's Rules

1. No judgment of ideas is permitted in the meeting. No member of the group is allowed to criticize any idea proposed by another member.

2. Wildness is encouraged. The crazier the idea, the better. It is easier to tone down an idea than to think one up.

3. Quantity of ideas is desired. The more ideas that are proposed, the greater the chances of finding winners.

4. Improvement of ideas is sought. In addition to contributing ideas of their own, the group members are encouraged to suggest how another member's idea can be made better, or how two ideas can be combined into one super idea (known as piggy-backing).

Although the brainstorming session has an atmosphere of spontaneity, a successful meeting requires sufficient pre-planning. John Caples recommends these additional steps to ensure a profitable meeting:

■ Identify exactly the problem to be addressed.

■ Schedule the meeting well in advance to see that all creative members can attend. Choose a time and place when your group will not be interrupted.

■ Write a memo stating the problem accompanied with a brief background of the situation. This allows the creative team to begin mulling their ideas so the meeting will not start cold.

■ Set a time limit for the meeting well within the average person's attention span. Set the duration of the meeting from about 20 to 45 minutes – no longer. It's like the principle of the reciprocity of film. The longer it takes to develop the ideas the slower the ideas will come.

■ Keep a complete and accurate account of all the ideas

generated, and make that list available to those specific people involved with the project.

■ Initiate action. Have the creative team begin to develop those ideas immediately while the ideas generated are still fresh.

■ The person chairing the meeting enforces the rules of the meeting. Furthermore, he or she should prevent any one person from dominating the discussion. The chairperson should refrain from giving personal ideas until the end of the meeting or unless there's a lull and a new idea might spark new interest.

5. How to write a memo

I'm sure you never expected to read that the successful art director should be able to write a coherent memo. It's for that very reason that it's included here. A memo is an internal message for other members of the company. The purpose of the memo as it concerns art directors is three-fold:

1. To inform. In the midst of a project you may want to keep other members of the agency aware of its progress. This is a good practice, especially within a large agency where you may not see some people for days at a time. It's also a way of informing superiors about existing or potential problems. At a smaller agency this type of memo may not be necessary, as you will probably meet others during the day.

2. For purposes of documentation. With any company problems concerning employees, suppliers, or clients, these issues should be documented. It's advisable to document significant conversations – telephone or otherwise – whenever the status of the job has changed or difficulties arise. An internal memo is a property of the agency and can be used as legal evidence in a court of law, if ever it comes to that. The memo should be distributed to the account person, creative director and any associated with the account or the project. Be sure to write this memo immediately.

Heed the words of the late Sam Ervin. While chastising a defendant about his less than scrupulous documentation of the events of surrounding the Watergate break-in, Senator Ervin proposed, "One scratch of the pen is worth more than all the slippery recollections of many witnesses."

3. To initiate action. A memo is like a runner's starting blocks, a starting point from where a runner can push off for further action. Writing makes ideas, information, directives, etc., concrete, giving the recipient something tangible to react to. It also makes requests less likely to be forgotten.

What makes an effective memo? An effective memo is one that gets read – no easy task when you consider the ever increasing glut of paperwork generated in today's business world. To get read a memo must be:

- **Attention getting.** Throw away all those misconceptions that memos have to be boring to be businesslike. As with advertising, the greatest crime is to be dull. Try to make your memo a grabber from the start.

- **Well written.** T'aint no way any no account type personage is goin' to give that there memo a read over if it's not done written proper where the grammer ain't too polished. (Poor grammatically structured memos are difficult to read). Take as much care as you can in your sentence structure, spelling and punctuation.

- **Brief.** Try to keep your memo less than a page in length. This will increase the chances of having it read.

- **Direct/To the point.** State your objective in the first sentence if possible.

■ **Beneficial.** "What's in it for me" That's what the reader wants to know. Give the reader a reason to read it quickly. Let the reader know why this information is important.

■ **Specific.** If you're writing about an employee disciplinary problem, outline the specifics. If you're arranging for a photo shoot let the client know the exact time, date and place. If there's a problem situation with a supplier, relate the chronological order of events. Details add credibility to your memo.

■ **Prompt action.** Tell the reader what the next course of action should be and who will be responsible to act.

6. How to estimate a job

The art director is often called upon to estimate the cost of producing advertising: mechanicals, photography, artwork, even television production, often upwards of $100,000.

With that in mind I don't think I need to elaborate on the importance of accurate, and well thought out production estimates. However, I will give you some pointers on how to ensure the accuracy of your estimate.

1. Before you contact your suppliers spend time reviewing the ad inch by inch, and the commercial frame by frame. Consider all aspects of the production. I've also found it helpful to review the job with the account executive who may present concerns you may have overlooked. Write down all the particulars.

2. Obtain at least three bids on large projects whether it's from photographers or TV production houses. Be sure to explain to the supplier all the various details, omitting nothing. To make sure they have a clear understanding of the project, ask them how they intend to execute the production from several suppliers. Be suspicious if you find a large discrepancy in prices. Somebody obviously doesn't understand the project.

3. Keep in mind that the lowest price may not always be the best value. You may accept the smaller bid and then discover the results don't meet the client's standards. Remember this: Clients never forget a poor job, no matter how much they saved.

4. Use a production estimate form. Utilize a form to help you allow for all variables. I've provided the form on Page 78 that I use for estimating print production (other than the actual printing quote).

5. Be conservative in your estimate – don't cut the estimate so close that there's no margin for error. It's better to over estimate and look like a hero when the job comes in under budget, than to go over budget and appear incompetent when you have to ask the client for more money. Ouch! Also, make allowances for the inevitable time and expense revisions add to a job.

6. Once your estimate is complete have your estimator and the account person review it for accuracy. And, of course, add the agency commission.

Now you know six things every art director should know, you're six ways closer to being the successful art director you want to be.

Production Estimate Sheet

CREATIVE

Copy	_____ hrs. @$_____ per hour =	$_____
Copy Revision	_____ hrs. @$_____ per hour =	$_____
Subtotal		$_____
Creative Supervision	_____ hrs. @$_____ per hour =	$_____
Concept development	_____ hrs. @$_____ per hour =	$_____
Subtotal		$_____
Mechanical	_____ hrs. @$_____ per hour =	$_____
Mechanical Revision	_____ hrs. @$_____ per hour =	$_____
Ordering Stats	_____ hrs. @$_____ per hour =	$_____
Specing Type	_____ hrs. @$_____ per hour =	$_____
Subtotal		$_____

ART AND PHOTOGRAPHY

Illustration	$_____
Photography	$_____
Film Polaroids	$_____
Processing	$_____
Subtotal	$_____
Retouching	$_____
Stats/Film	$_____
Models	$_____
Clothes	$_____
Makeup	$_____
Subtotal	$_____
Stylist	$_____
Props	$_____
Prep	$_____
Model Construction	$_____
Subtotal	$_____
Food Stylist	$_____
Food	$_____
Food Shop/Prep	$_____
Subtotal	$_____

PRINT PRODUCTION

Type	$_____
Color Separation	$_____
Photo makeup	$_____

MISCELLANEOUS

Transportation	$_____
Travel	_____ miles @_____ ¢ per mile = $_____
Postage	$_____

GRAND TOTAL

CHAPTER VI

Art Directing and Photography

The Big Picture

If there's a choice between running photography or illustration in an ad or a brochure, I tend to side with photography. Photography is real. Consumers instinctively know that the camera records things as they really are – that "the camera never lies." It's a powerful medium for demonstrating products as well as services. The fact is, research has shown photography is 26% more effective than illustrations for selling the same products or services.

A Photograph's Effectiveness Can Depend On Three Factors:

1. Stopping power.

Photography can grab a person's attention and keep it. The visual, the photograph or illustration, is usually the first visual element the reader sees in an ad. If a photo is dull, uninteresting, or confusing, don't expect your audience to stick around to read the copy. Effective photography can arouse your reader's curiosity and lead them right into the copy.

No one will disagree a photo of a naked woman or man has stopping power. But more often a photo's stopping power has "story appeal." For instance, the businessman caught in mid-flight along with his American Tourister luggage, after being side-swiped by an automobile. Or the chimpanzee standing next to an office copier. Immediately the reader asks, "What's going on here?" The audience is compelled to read the copy explaining that the luggage survived the real life accident, or the copier is so easy to operate that a chimp can master it.

2. Teamwork.

When photography and copy work together successfully you get winning advertising. The photograph should illustrate and complement the headline. As an example, we see a man attempting to stuff an arm chair in a washing machine. An intriguing but absurd image, you would say. But put it together with a headline: "You wish," and it becomes an effective ad for an upholstery cleaner. It's important to think of photography, headline and copy as a team, working together, scoring more sales for the client.

3. Feature the product.

The photography should show the product or service. Even the Infinity car ads eventually came around to show the product. People like to see what they're buying. Particularly, Missourians. They're always saying, "Show me." If your product lends itself to demonstration in photography, show it.

Jimmy Olson to Richard Avedon:
Choosing the right photographer

You've developed the concept. The client has bought the idea. You're ready to produce the ad. Now it's time to select a photographer for the job. Try to select the photographer best for your client, the product or service, and, of course, the budget.

Keep this criteria in mind when you're making your selection:

1. Style. Every photographer will have his or her own strengths. Some are good at tabletop. Others excel at fashion and portraiture. Some work better in the studio, others on location. This one uses traditional lighting, another goes for special effects. It all comes down to how you'd like to see the ad executed.

2. Budget. "I was at my desk when the AE suddenly burst into my office and announced, 'The client wants an awarding-winning brochure. Spare no expense. Especially the photography. Get Scavullo if you have to, but make this piece sing!...' And then I woke up."

It's rare when money is no object. The budget will often determine which photographer you use. Then, again, perhaps the photographer you prefer to use is slow right now and will do your job for a lower fee. If you're a steady customer, he or she might be glad to help you out.

3. Complexity of the shot. Are you simply shooting a glass of soda, or are you capturing an exploding bottle of champagne? Is it a picture of a model against a seamless background, or a rock guitarist clutching his instrument, while floating above a dreamscape of pyramids and a sphinx. Some photographers are adept at organizing and coordinating special effects and large productions; others are not.

4. Experience. You might not know to bring a camera polarizing filter when doing aerial photography. Or that it's necessary to bring a bottle of Armor–All when shooting cars or trucks. That's why it pays to select a photographer who's "been there before."

5. Availability. If your preferred photographer is booked on another shoot for the local dairy, the other considerations regarding the choice of photographer become moot. But again, if you're a good account perhaps the photographer will re-arrange his schedule to accommodate you.

I might consider two photographers for a single job if, let's say, the cover of a brochure requires an elaborate table top display but the rest of the brochure calls for location shooting.

Be demanding. There are basic expectations I have of any photographer. I expect the photographer to produce an accurate representation of the layout, proper exposure, quick delivery, all at a reasonable price. Furthermore I would encourage the photographer to make suggestions, enhancing the shot in such a way that he or she infuse the photograph with life. Ninety-nine percent of the time I'll provide the photographer with a layout. Occasionally, I will ask for just a pure and simple attention-grabbing special effect, and look to the photographer for the answer.

Plan your photo session using a photography checklist. Before I contact the photographer, I fill out my photography checklist. (See page 83). This list addresses all the various items to be considered when planning a photo session, and getting an accurate price quote. This laundry list accounts for such things as number of shots, whether the shoot will be on location or in the studio, will be black and white or in color, will models be necessary, etc.

Some things to consider when reviewing the checklist:

Copyright. I make it clear to all photographers from the outset that my clients must have control over all copyrights, including ownership and all reproduction rights. While obtaining the copyright privilege may increase the photographer's fee slightly, it's generally worth the cost to the client. Owning the copyright gives the client the right to use and reproduce the photography where they want and as often as they want, without the permission of the photographer.

Short of complete copyright ownership, some photographers are now offering unlimited usage, for limited periods of time, say six months to 3 years. Even though my client retains the copyright I suggest that photographers be allowed to reproduce their work for self-promotion purposes. For more on copyright laws see chapter entitled "Miscellaneous Matters."

Film Format. The bigger the format the sharper the image, and the more you can enlarge the image. The format you shoot will depend on how large the photo will reproduce. If the main shot appears in a full page ad, I would go with 4x5. 8x10 format for two page spreads in

PHOTOGRAPHY CHECK LIST

Client_____**Job Name**_____ **Job#** _____
Photographer _____Day Rate $_____
  Copyright fee $_____❏ No copyright desired
Photographer _____Day Rate $_____
  Copyright fee $ _____❏ No copyright desired
Number of days shooting____Agency rep._____
Film Black and white   ❏ Color
    Format ❏ 35mm ❏ 2 1/4 ❏ 4 x 5 ❏ 8 x 10
    ❏ Transparency ❏ Negatives ❏ Prints (size) _____
    ❏ Polaroids – ❏ Black and white ❏ Color
    Processing handled by ❏ agency ❏ photographer
    ❏ Studio ❏ On location
    Travel expenses____# of miles @_____¢ per mile
    Cost of Processing $_____
Food Stylist _____ Day Rate $ _____
  Prep day rate $ _____
Stylist _____Day Rate $ _____
  Prep day rate $ _____
Props:
    1._____ 2._____3._____ 4._____
    5._____6._____7._____ 8._____
Prop/model maker_____Fee $_____
    1._____ 2._____
Graphics ❏ Art/Graphic ❏ Labels ❏ Identacolor ❏ Backgrounds
❏ **Retouching** _____Fee $_____
Models:
  Agency _____Name_____ Fee $_____
  Agency _____Name_____Fee $_____
  Agency _____Name_____Fee $_____
  Clothes:
    1._____ 2._____ 3._____ 4._____
    5._____6._____7._____ 8._____
  ❏ Model Release forms
❏ **Make-up artist** _____ Fee $ _____
Shot List:
    1._____2._____ 3._____ 4._____
    5._____6._____7._____ 8._____
❏ **Express Delivery** $_____

magazines and brochures, up to poster size reproduction. 2¼ x 2¼ format film if the shot is a smaller inset, or if your subject is a moving subject and you intend to shoot a great number of shots in rapid succession, such as fashion photography, a sporting event, or a machine working. 35mm is also acceptable for action photography and especially useful when shooting on location. It can also be ideal when used for editorial type shots where larger format equipment would be obtrusive and cumbersome to set up.

Film and processing. This is probably the smallest expense in relation to the job as a whole. That's why I always tell my photographers to shoot as much film as necessary and to bracket their shots (shooting slightly darker and lighter, in addition to those shots at the ideal exposure). I would rather invest in the minimal cost of film and processing than not shooting enough film, not getting the shot we want, and consequently having to reschedule a makeup shoot. And don't spare the Polaroid instant film, either. The photographer uses Polaroid to immediately determine the proper lighting set up and exact exposure before taking the final shot on film. During the course of the session, the photographer will take several Polaroids while fine tuning the shot. Some photographers, very few, but some, don't use Polaroid instant film, and then you have to request it. I swear by it. I'm so adamant about using Polaroid, and lots of it, photographers begin to think I own stock in the company. The fact is, I just appreciate being able to see as accurately as I can what I'm getting before the final film is taken.

Photographers feel comfortable using black and white Polaroid to determine the exposure and lighting, even when the final shot will be in color. Some believe color Polaroid film is too inaccurate. It's true, the color is off, always with a slightly greenish cast, but I think it gives me information that the black and white can't. And when I feel good about the way the color Polaroid looks, then I know the final shot is going to be spectacular (I think Freud called this obsessive compulsive behavior).

Prop/photo stylists. Usually the photographer will be willing to gather props if needed – a plate or cup here, a lamp there. But if the shot requires hard to find props or the list of props is extensive, the photographer and the AD may find it beneficial to call in a photo stylist. The photo stylist's job is to gather and coordinate the props for the shot. Their job can be extremely important. How they prop will determine the whole look and feel of the photography.

The prop stylist will not only gather the props, but he or she will work with the photographer on the set arranging the items. Having the stylist on the set also gives you the option of last minute changes and gathering additional props.

You'll want to meet with the prop stylist at least a week before the shoot to discuss the layout and reach an understanding regarding the style of the shot. The type and number of props will vary. The stylist may need to gather place settings for a food shot. Other times, it may mean furniture for an entire room.

Stylists will generally arrange the rental of certain props. Often the stylist will have to buy the props outright and you'll have to reimburse them, although the stylist should inform you of the price of any significant purchases and get your okay.

Keep in mind you may need a separate stylist adept at buying clothes if you're employing models.

Food stylists. It takes years of training to become an accomplished professional food stylist (at one time known as home economists). Like sculptors when it comes to preparing food to be used in advertising photography, they're intimately familiar with the texture, pliability, and idiosyncrasies of different foods. More importantly, they also know that what whets the appetite of a hungry family doesn't necessarily make for an appealing shot thru the lens of a camera. They are the key person when it comes to food photography – much more important than even the photographer when it comes to the success of the shot.

Preparing food for photography is the art of idealizing

food; how to make it look perfect for the camera. Perfection to the food stylist is building the ideal chocolate brownie crumb by crumb because it doesn't have the right appetite appeal naturally as it comes from the oven. Or cooking over 1,000 pancakes to come up with enough that have a smooth contour and golden-brown color, as they do at General Mills' kitchens. Sometimes what looks appetizing may be completely inedible. For instance, did you know that Elmer's glue makes a great substitute for milk when shooting photography for the front of cereal packages? And that sometimes the ice cream you see in print ads is really Crisco shortening? These are just some of the food stylist's tricks of the trade.

The food stylist is paid on a par with a prop stylist, although the food stylist may charge a lower rate when it comes to prep time; that is, going out to gather the food necessary for the shot.

Both food and prop stylists are the best investments to ensure the success of the shoot. The costs of their services are minimal compared to, let's say, the photographer's fee.

Model makers. Sometimes you may find it necessary to have models or props made. For example, I had the experience working for a turkey meat processor. Often some unsightly fat or water would surface after manufacturing in between the meat and the packaging; a natural result of the process. We spent untold hours with the food stylist and considerable money on computer retouching to correct the problem – all with less than satisfactory results. Finally we convinced the client to have a model made of his product. The model maker sculpted a replica of the product, cast it in acrylic and painted it, thus eliminating the problem for all future photo sessions.

On another occasion we were planning to shoot an office scene, but rather than scouting out locations and losing control over lighting by working outside the photographer's studio, we had a prop maker construct a miniature office that was convincing enough to keep it in the background of the photograph.

Models are useful and necessary for products that aren't yet in production; or for special effects like freezing action, such as pouring paint; or creating a 3-D version of the client's logo, and so forth. The cost of making a model will vary widely based on the complexity of the model, the cost of the materials, and the amount of time it takes to manufacture.

Models. Most models are represented by agencies. You call the agency requesting a model and give them a brief description in terms of age, physical characteristics, and possibly characterization. I've found it helpful to write down all the characteristics of the model before contacting the model agency. The form on Page 88 will help in this process. At that time you'll also arrange to have the models stop at your location for an interview. Good models know their strengths and weaknesses, how to work with the camera and are receptive to suggestions and direction.

Once you've interviewed the selection of models and settled on one, you contact the agency and relate the details of the shoot, i.e. date, place, wardrobe requirements. The price of models will vary widely depending on your market, the looks of the model, their experience, how long you plan to use the model, how far the model has to travel to the photography studio and especially how "in demand" the model is.

Generally you can hire a model for between $65 and $125 an hour throughout America, except for perhaps New York and L.A. where well-known models are paid up to $3000 a day and more. On top of that there's the agency fee (a percentage of the model's fee), and travel time, if any, which is calculated at about 50% of the modeling hourly fee.

Make-up artists. Professional models often know how to apply their own basic makeup and may even carry a simple makeup kit with them. But you certainly shouldn't hire a high paid fashion model without also using a makeup artist. That's like baking a birthday cake and forgetting the candles. Makeup artists also may work well with amateurs such as office workers. They can take the

Model/Talent Checklist

Number of Models_____
❑ Male____# ❑ Female____#
Age(s)_____,_____,_____
Race(s)_____,_____,_____
❑ Hand Model
Build: ❑ Muscular ❑ Slender ❑ Medium
Acting ability ❑ Yes ❑ Not necessary
Height:_____ft._____in.
Weight:_____lbs.
Measurement   Bust_____in.
              Hips_____in.
              Waist_____in.
              Shoe Size_____
              Hat Size_____
Hair ❑ Blonde ❑ Brown ❑ Black ❑ Redhead ❑ Other
Eyes ❑ Green ❑ Brown❑ Blue❑ Gray ❑ Doesn't matter
Length of time needed_____hrs._____days
Location of photosession_____
Hourly fee $_____Total Cost $_____

most humdrum business people and add a degree of star quality with makeup.

Makeup for film and photography differs from that of the stage. The camera is so revealing, the makeup for photography must be more subtle and less opaque than stage makeup. Photography is two dimensional and tends to flatten a person's features, and add weight. That's great for skinny models, but heavy models require more makeup to define their faces. Makeup counteracts this and regains form through the use of light and dark makeup and color. Most times, the makeup artist will brush on some pancake makeup and dust the shiny spots off the nose and forehead concentrating on overall facial definition, covering blemishes and generally enhancing a person's looks. Other times, it may mean applying more dramatic character makeup – moustache, coloring hair, a new nose – and may require a specialist in this area.

Often budgets don't allow for a professional makeup artist. There are also times when the makeup requirements are minimal. It's times like these you may decide to learn more about basic makeup yourself. Instructional books are available and you can find supplies in costume and dance supply shops.

Details. It's the little details that you overlook when putting together the estimate that will come back to haunt you – when the final cost of the photography is tallied and you discover you're over budget. For instance, rush charges for film processing; the slight retouching that was unexpected, but necessary; the charge for an assistant that the photographer failed to mention; and the fact that the shoot went half a day over because of poor planning. You can't anticipate all these circumstances. Furthermore, to account for every possibility would put the estimate sky-high. Here, experience and pre-planning count.

Once I work out the details using the photography checklist, either I meet with the photographer(s) in person or fax a copy of the layout and discuss the particulars over the phone. The photographer may offer to coordinate with the various other talents for the shoot – the makeup artist, stylist, etc. – at no extra cost to you. Often I have a good idea which photographer would be right for the job, and therefore won't bother bidding the job with several photographers. I ask for a written estimate, detailing the various costs involved. After the estimate is approved by the client it's time to arrange for the photo session.

The importance of the pre-production meeting.

This is a good opportunity to make sure all the bases have been covered and there is complete agreement as to what's expected from all parties.

Those attending the pre-production meeting should be the art director, the photographer, and perhaps the account executive. Invite the client if it seems appropriate. You'll want to cover things like starting time. Who will bring what. Is the client to bring the product? What type of background material? Does the photographer foresee any difficulties executing the shot?

You may already know the answer to many of these questions, but the purpose of the pre-production session is to arrive at a meeting of the minds of everybody involved.

The Session

The day has finally arrived. The models are on their way, the makeup artist is laying out an assortment of cosmetic products, the food stylist is busy cooking, the prop stylist is arranging several place settings, while the photographer's assistants are loading film and lighting the set. But, for the art director the photography session is a waiting game. Here, patience isn't only a virtue, it's a necessity.

You will spend interminable hours waiting for everyone else involved to complete their tasks before you can finally put your stamp of approval on the proceedings. The art director must keep constant vigil over the photo session. The food stylist will need to know if you prefer the garbanzo beans or the olives as a garnish. The makeup artist will ask if the models will require day or evening makeup, the models will have a selection of clothes from which you must choose, etc. All that, in addition to working with the photographer to make sure the lighting, background and camera angle are correct.

Sooner or later every art director learns these two unbreakable axioms regarding the photo sessions:

Rule 1. Photo sessions will take as long as they take, and...

Rule 2. Photo sessions always take a long time.

My style is to stay involved, but only to a point. I don't need to know how the photographer plans to mount lighting, or the exact method for accomplishing a special effect. However, I don't have any hesitation about looking through the lens to see if the angle is representative of the layout, or suggesting a smooth, more even lighting effect as opposed to harsher, directional lighting.

Other art directors may have a more "whatever goes" attitude. They feel it's important not to stifle the photographer's creative impulses; that photographers need to express themselves. My thoughts are:

1. Art directors are not paid to be patrons of the arts. They are paid to represent the agency and their clients.

2. When clients approve a layout, they are approving that particular layout and not just the photographer's interpretation of the layout. If you want to explore creative options, do so at the planning/layout stage before presentation to the client. Meet with the photographer at the concept stage or just prior to layout to get his or her input.

3. At the photo session you can allow the photographer to shoot the layout any way he or she wants, but only after the shot for the layout is "in the can."

How to prepare. To be effective at the photo session, it's important to be prepared. Here is a list of items I usually bring to any photo session:

■ **Photographer's loupe** – A magnifier used to review Polaroids to inspect details in the shot

■ **Rubber cement** – For gluing labels, or other uses when you might need to adhere objects together firmly

■ **Tracing pad** – Good for visualizing ideas on the set

■ **Proportion wheel** – For making sure the photo will fit the ad properly when it blows up

■ **Flair pens** – Or pencils. You will have to write with something

■ **Artist Markers** – Broad and fine nib for touch up on the set

■ **Exacto knife and blades** – More accurate than scissors for cutting apart Polaroids to see how different elements will be pieced together in the final printed ad or brochure

■ **Ruler** – Use it as a cutting guide, as a drawing aid and for measuring when using the proportion wheel

Once everything is arranged in front of the camera it's a matter of taking Polaroids, refining the details, arranging props and lighting until you, the photographer, and the client (if present) are satisfied. Then, the photographer shoots the final film.

Photo Session Etiquette. Just as too many cooks spoil the broth (food stylists withstanding), too many "art directors" spoil the shoot. One art director should run the photo session. If the client or account executive are on the set, they should direct all their comments to the art director and the art director should forward that information to the photographer, food stylist, makeup person, etc. This should be made clear before the session begins. This also applies to creative directors. If the agency creative director wants to direct the shoot, fine, but one person should take responsibility before the shoot begins.

Delay breaking down the set once the shoot is over, just in case of the rare, unfortunate situation where the photography has to be redone because the shots were taken incorrectly, the film was defective, the film processing lab destroys the film, or many other reasons.

When the unfortunate does occur, don't be devastated. The photographs may be under or over exposed! The color balance is way off! The batch of film from the manufacturer was faulty! The lab misplaced your job! What to do?

First, determine who exactly is responsible. If it's the manufacturer's fault, you might as well go whistling in the wind. They might reimburse you for the film, small consolation when you've spent thousands on the spoiled shot.

However, a professional photographer won't leave this to chance. Good photographers buy their film in bulk and test one roll or several sheets of film for quality. Before you use a photographer for the first time you might inquire if he or she bothers to take this precautionary step. If you don't ask, and they don't do it, you could be headed for trouble.

If the lab is responsible you have no more recourse than you do with the manufacturer. However, any lab with a reputation for carelessness is on the road to bankruptcy.

In the end, it's the photographer who takes the burden if he or she doesn't deliver the shot. You shouldn't be expected to pay for the shoot a second time (Of course, I'd play it safe and have the photographer sign a contract specifying who's responsible for what). If you've paid the entire costs of the first shoot, then you can ask the photographer to handle the entire burden of rearranging for another photo session, pay for the costs of any food stylist, prop stylist, film, and donate his or her time.

A Variety of Assignments

Work long enough in advertising and you'll encounter just about every type of photographic subject there is. Each has its own challenges and pitfalls.

Food. The food stylist counts for 90% of the success when it comes to food photography. Generally, the food stylist will make up food as a "stand-in," something like an actor's double, early in the shoot to allow the photographer to arrange lighting, background, and to take test Polaroids before the final food is prepared.

Food is something you can't rush. Usually everyone will be standing around waiting for the food stylist to complete his or her preparations. But when it's finally brought onto the set, heaven help you. Food tends to spoil quickly. At least for photographic purposes, it does. You normally have about 20 minutes from the time the food is brought out under the lights before lettuce begins to turn tobacco leaf brown, and the hamburger takes on the characteristics of synthetic rubber.

Be sure to have plenty of product on hand, to the point of absurdity. You'll probably use it. I recall one occasion where we deep fried three cases of chicken fingers till we discovered the one with just the right curves, the most inviting bread crumbs, the ideal length, and the most exquisite coloring. Now, that chicken finger had star quality!

Even using professional photographers and food stylists, there's no insurance against having to retouch. It's wise to always budget for retouching. The general rule of thumb (my thumb that is) states that retouching should be estimated at 50% of the cost of the photographer.

Industrial. Shooting on location for industrial clients is a far cry from the comfortable, predictable surroundings of the photographer's studio. By industrial I mean such subject matter as a window manufacturing plant, a UPS shipping depot, a waterfront pier, a waste water processing facility, a pharmaceutical processing company, etc. It takes a special calibre of photographer to go into a deep, dark, dingy, dirty industrial complex and come out with photography that, at times, can look downright beautiful. I know only a handful of such photographers and they are worth their weight in gold. If you doubt what can be done in such a setting, take a look at the work of famous Life magazine photographer, Margaret Bourke-White.

The special talent of an industrial photographer is to arrive at the site (site unseen), size up the situation and start arranging lighting immediately. It's not a bowl of cherries.

■ **Factories are often large and dimly lit.** They require a tremendous amount of photographic lighting. Color balance is also a problem as a factory may have half a dozen shades of fluorescent lighting.

■ **The site may be dirty.** You may find yourself along with the photographer policing the area.

■ **Photography can be intrusive and interfere with the manufacturing process.** As a result, you may find the plant foreman to be less than helpful and sometimes out and out uncooperative.

■ **Space is often at a premium.** Be prepared to shoot in tight corners with few if any electrical outlets nearby.

■ **Sometimes industrial photography can be downright dangerous.** There may be occasions where a shot has to be taken from great heights, or near hazardous machinery. There are even unseen dangers that only the experienced photographer can foresee, such as the chemical plant where fumes could easily ignite from the flash of a strobe light.

Business-to-business. Often photography for business-to-business communication looks pretty much the same. You have your choice of showing a picture of the company headquarters, the obligatory portrait of the president, the customer service department fielding phone calls, the company group picture, the company computer shot, or all of the above.

The set will be some person's office or the conference room and you won't have the necessary time for elaborate setup and lighting. You'll probably even be cleaning up the work space to make it look organized. The models will be company employees, although you get the feeling you're looking at a bunch of runaways from a mannequin convention. The key is to be flexible and be ready to work with the photographer to accomplish the shots.

The role of the art director in shooting business-to-business photography is to pave the way for the photographer, coordinate the shooting schedule and act as the liaison between the photographer and the client's company.

Many times I've purposely hired PR and newspaper photographers for business-to-business photography because they're used to working in this kind of setting. They can go into an office, determine the best, most dramatic angle, set up quickly, take the shot and then move on.

Fashion. Fashion photography is by far the most glamorous and sought after art direction accounts there are. And when the average model charges anywhere from $100 to $300 an hour they're usually the shortest photo sessions. With that in mind, it's good to prepare fully before the models arrive, making sure that all the details of lighting, background, costume, and makeup have been worked out ahead of time.

Good fashion photographers are a mystery. Call it chemistry, call it psychology – they have the ability to put models at ease, and to create an atmosphere of spontaneity, bringing out the best in models.

More often than not the models will be shot in motion, where the key is to shoot fast, using plenty of film. At the same time make sure the photographer doesn't ignore the model's clothes. If a dress starts to buckle, or a suit becomes wrinkled and looks displeasing, stop momentarily to straighten or iron them. It would be a pity if your model strikes the perfect pose only to have the hem of her skirt riding up.

Model release form. I have also included a model release form on Page 98 for your convenience. You'd be surprised how many photographers don't keep these on hand. Whether you're using a professional model or an amateur, it's important to use this form. Without it a person in a photograph can prevent or limit the use of the photograph after it's taken. Strictly speaking, everyone, professional or amateur, who appears in a photograph and is recognizable, even if they appear in the distant background, must sign a model release form. Furthermore, merely signing the release form is not enough. To make this contract legal there must be an exchange, or as a lawyer would say, "consideration for services rendered" to make the contract binding. In the case of amateurs the consideration need only be $1.

Some other points to consider:

Retouching – It's a matter of pride with photographers not to have to retouch their photography. And I would be suspect of any photographer who recommended retouching as a solution to a problem that could easily be handled with a little extra time and care in lighting and arranging the product. Sure, great strides have been made in photo retouching, especially with the use of computers at the separation stage, but they are only so good, aside from being a costly remedy.

Trick of the trade – If type placement is critical to your layout, you can employ this simple method. Take your layout, make a line drawing of the ad including showing placement of the type and headline. Then make a positive film stat reduced to fit the 4x5 or 2¼ ground glass for the photographer to use on his or her camera. The photographer can thereby accurately frame the shot without the fear of type running into the visual.

Photographers want tear sheets – Photographers greatly appreciate having printed samples or tear sheets of the ads they've worked on, even if they don't request it. Same for models. You'll be helping them keep their

Model Release and Permission

I_____hereby accept the payment
of_____dollar(s), and for this consideration I
hereby irrevocably consent to and authorize the use and
reproduction by you (the agency), your clients or assigns, of
any and all photographs which have been taken this day of
me, by you or your duly authorized photographer. Negatives
and prints, transparencies, or proofs, which may be hereto
attached, may be used for any purpose whatsoever without
further compensation to me or my assigns. All negatives and
positives, as well as prints and other forms of reproduction are
hereby assigned to you, your clients and assigns, and shall
constitute your property solely and completely,

Date_____ Model's age (if a minor)_____
Model's signature _____
Model's Name _____
Address_____
Phone(_____)_____
Signature of Parent or Guardian

_____
Agency_____
Client_____Job_____
Witness_____

portfolios up to date, and it's not bad advertising for your work either.

Effective use of stock photography – I used to equate the use of stock photography with clip art. It's true that a lot of stock photography is very mundane and predictable. Often though, it can be the perfect solution. I don't think I could pay a photographer enough, at least not the ones that I know, to stand in the curl of a mountainous ocean wave with their expensive Hasselblads in hand. Yet, when I needed just such a shot, there it was in a stock photography catalog.

Today there are a number of good national stock photography houses, each with an extensive library of images. There are also houses like FPG and the Bettmann Archives that specialize in period photos, photos of historic events and famous people.

Most of the larger houses work in a similar manner. When you request a photo, they will initiate a search and charge you a fee to wade through their vast libraries of material. The fee runs about $75 and has to be paid whether or not they find the photo you need. If they do have a photo to your liking, they will apply the search fee to the final cost of photo usage.

Stock photo houses charge using a formula based on usage (poster, ad, brochure), the audience (trade, consumer, associations) and the number of impressions or circulation. And the greater the number of the uses the lower the fee per use, the more cost effective the stock photography becomes. I've also discovered recently that a number of the photographers I already use have their own collection of stock which they make available at a lower rate than stock houses and without a research fee.

You can even obtain free stock photography if you're ready to do a little detective work. The truth is the greatest library of free stock photography is the federal and state governments. Photos from state parks, NASA, the Nation Weather Service, and more are all available to you, free. You, the tax payer, have already paid for it so you might as well use it. One very helpful guide is <u>The Directory of Free Stock Photography/2</u>, published by Infosource Business Publications. This handy book lists the agencies, and departments that keep photo files, what subject matter they have, even the contact person's name.

In Closing

As an art director, no one expects you to get behind the camera and snap the shutter. That's why you hire competent photographers. But it's not healthy to stay ignorant, either. If you have a fair idea of what can and can not be accomplished on film, you will no doubt be better equipped to art direct photographers. If you're not already acquainted with photography I recommend you read several books or take a course. Learn how a large format bellows camera works, how to look at negatives, become familiar with the basic types of film available, and their different quality color balance, the variety of basic lighting set-ups, etc.

Once you become comfortable with this information and you've attended several shoots, the practices outlined here will become second nature and art directing advertising photography will be a snap.

CHAPTER VII

Coping with the Graphics Computer

The computer in no way signals the death of the art director or the graphic designer. It is a tool – like pencils, markers, graphics pads, parallel rules, etc. – albeit an incredibly fast, powerful and accurate tool. But it still takes the genius of the artist to create a design.

In the last several years, the graphics computer has matured and is now becoming the standard in the industry, while computer graphics is part of the everyday curriculum at many colleges and art schools. What I have to say in one chapter will not answer all of your questions about computers as it relates to graphic design. You may even finish this chapter slightly more confused than when you started. Don't worry. Give yourself time.

Start by subscribing to one or two computer magazines. At first, you may find it difficult to make any sense of all the jargon, but you'll pick it up eventually.

Next, attend computer seminars and demonstrations. It seems every computer store or manufacturer is holding one these days. Call several computer stores to find out when these events will be held in your area.

Most larger cities have graphics conventions or expos at least once a year – make it a point to attend.

Ask plenty of questions. Expect to get plenty of "I don't knows." This is all so new, there are few people who really have a complete command of graphic computers. And if you still find all of this too overwhelming, you might even consider hiring a computer consulting firm. Not surprisingly, they're becoming popular.

Finally, you're going to lay your money down and buy the computer. It's only then will you begin to understand fully what a graphics computer is all about.

The Graphics Computer – It's Functions. For the art director the graphics computer functions in two ways. First, as an aid in design and layout. Second, as a means of producing complete mechanicals on screen, without ever having to paste-down a single piece of type on a board.

Using the computer as a design tool, you can effectively manipulate all those elements of type, art, line art, logos, tonal backgrounds, spot color and photography, all without moving out of your seat.

Then at the push of a button you can print your layout in black & white or full color, ready for presentation to your client. Or you can go so far as producing finished mechanicals complete with crop marks and position stats on one piece of repro paper, with no sacrifice in quality.

There are also software programs available to manipulate separations made by your color separator, allowing you to strip together your own four color separations, thus eliminating stripping charges from your color separator or printer.

With the graphics computer, layouts are nearly as accurate as a mechanical. Furthermore, with the proper equipment you can even output a layout using a color printer – the result, a high fidelity comp indicating spot color, color background and type, along with full color photos. Thus eliminating the use of color markers.

So you say you're computer illiterate? Well, you don't have to be a computer programmer to operate these machines. The current crop of computers are so user friendly, you can be up and running (with a minimum amount of training), composing your own layouts and mechanicals within two or three weeks, even if you've never touched a computer keyboard before.

And don't worry if you're unfamiliar with the inner working of computers – you know, silicon chips and binary bits; I wouldn't give it a nano seconds concern. Peter A McWillaims in his book, <u>The Personal Computer Book</u>, lends his perspective. He says it's curious that we find those National Geographic TV specials on the human body so fascinating "even though we've been successfully operating our bodies for years without all those microscopic, time-lapsed, animation-enhanced [special effects]."* The same applies to the computer.

Getting to know the computer system

First, let's get acquainted with the graphic computer system. Let's start with the basics.

The Computer – Consider the computer like a family photo album; it's where your memories are kept. For the art director the computer is where all your layouts, pictures, type and mechanicals will be stored.

Outwardly, the graphics computer is very much like any other computer, but there is a big difference, although it escapes me at the moment...Oh yes, it has to do with memory. Whereas typing letters and words on a computer dedicated to simple word processing is a relatively simple task, the amount of information a computer for graphics has to handle and remember – pictures, typefaces, layouts, illustrations, logos, etc. – is tremendous, requiring a large memory and storage capacity.

The Monitor – The beauty of the graphics computer is that you can see exactly how your composition, along with typefaces, will actually appear on screen. Monitors come in black & white, and color models. With a smaller monitor you can compose a single page, while a 19" will permit you to compose a two-page spread. You'll also hear the term grey scale in terms of black and white monitors. This

*The Personal Computer Book, Peter A McWilliams, Prelude Press, 1982

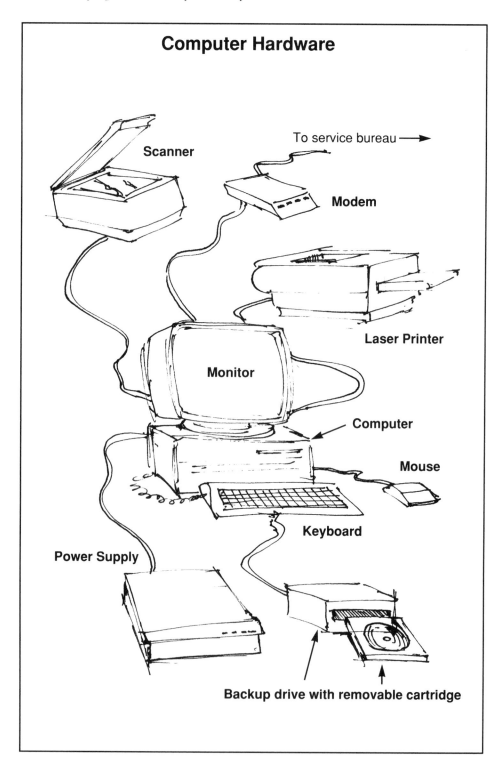

Computer Hardware

Scanner

To service bureau ⟶

Modem

Laser Printer

Monitor

Computer

Mouse

Keyboard

Power Supply

Backup drive with removable cartridge

will allow you to see and print a full range of tones and photographs.

The Keyboard – This is not only used to do word processing, but also to enter commands.

The Laser Printer – A low resolution proofing device to see on paper what is on the screen, before you go to the expense of having the job set on photographic paper. The proofs from the laser are extremely accurate and can be used for presentation to the client.

Along with this essential hardware is a number of peripheral pieces of equipment:

The Mouse – So named because of it's appearance; the mouse serves several functions. **1**. The mouse is a drawing tool. As you roll the mouse around on a special mouse rolling surface, or pad, you'll notice a corresponding cursor or scribe (which looks like this ➘) on the screen that mimics your movements with the mouse. Coordinating your hand with what appears on the screen takes some getting used to. **2**. The mouse is used for selecting commands from lists or "menus" that appear at the top of the screen. Under each menu you will be given a choice of commands to open to or create a new job, quit program, undo last command, enlarge the picture image, add color, and a long list of other commands. **3**. The mouse is used to compose elements on the page. With it, you determine where to place pictures, text, headlines, spot color, and much more.

The Scanner – With this device you can take a reflective picture or image and transfer it to your screen, at which point you can manipulate it — crop it, flop it, reverse it, etc. Scanners come in black and white, and color models and come with attachments to scan color slides.

The Modem – A handy piece of equipment which permits you to send jobs and information from one computer via telephone lines to other computers at various locations: client, printer, photo separator, or typehouse.

Imagesetter – After you have composed your job on screen and proofed it on the laser printer, you're ready to set your job on photographic repro quality paper or film. This is done through the use of an imagesetter, which uses light rays to expose the image created on the computer onto light sensitive paper. The paper is then run through a chemical processor to develop the image. Most image-setters are out of the price range for any single agency. That's why many typesetting companies now provide a service where they will take your floppy disk or your job over the modem and process the image for you at a minimal cost per page.

For your own protection I would also strongly recommend buying a:

Tape or Removable Cartridge Drive – All your work will be accomplished and stored in the computer on the hard drive, a large recording disk. Still, you should copy, or *back up*, all your work using a tape drive or removable cartridge drive. *Do this every day without fail at the end of the day*. All it takes is one hard drive malfunction and you've lost all the jobs stored in the computer. A tape drive will pay for itself in time it would otherwise take to recreate your lost files.

Power Supply – The power supply is your first line of defense against the problems of power outage during storms. The cost for this equipment is relatively insignificant compared to having to replace a hard disk full of art work and mechanicals.

No doubt you're wondering about the cost of all this modern technology. Well, let's just say it's less than the down payment on a house. But wait. Before you pull out your purchase order there's also the matter of software. There are literally thousands of types and brands of software for the graphics computer and the number is growing daily. Below are some of the basic types of programs you'll need for graphic design.

Three basic software programs

Desktop publishing software. This software allows you to compose your page incorporating text and headlines, and using boxes to indicate the position of photos and illustration. You can also indicate spot color, screen backgrounds, reverse type, and more. Furthermore, you can call up images – photography and illustration created in other software programs or from your scanner – and put them in place in your layout/mechanical.

Illustration software. It's doubtful you'll ever compete with accomplished illustrators using this software. But you will be able to easily achieve polished, illustrator quality results on simple spot illustrations, maps, diagrams, charts and other types of illustration.

Photo/illustration manipulation software. Once you've scanned in a picture or illustration you may want to manipulate it by changing the background, superimposing one image on another, airbrushing certain objects, or flopping an image. This, and more can all be done with this software. Although the image produced in this type of program is generally not of reproduction quality, it is still excellent for producing accurate comps and for indicating photo/illustration position and retouching for your separator or printer.

These are the most essential programs necessary to design on the computer, and day by day their powers and functions are being modified and improved. In addition, there is a myriad of peripheral and support software to expand the capabilities of your system, which you can add as the need arises.

Brand names. Although there are a number of entrants in the graphics computer game, the principal players are Macintosh and IBM. Judging from those people I polled informally, it would be safe to say that Macintosh owns about 99% of the graphics computer market. IBM has, until recently, had to play catch up when it comes to software. Now that's changed and the software packages available for both IBM and Mac computers are very similar. In addition, the two are comparable in computer speed, capabilities and equipment. Furthermore, if one develops an innovation, you know the other will be sure to follow shortly.

What the graphics computer will mean for you and your agency.

1. Changes in materials – The amount of artist's materials needed to create ads and layouts will be greatly reduced. I don't think you'll see the extinction of drawing pads and markers, but these will be used for preliminary design sketches whereas the computer will be used to produce more polished layout presentations. (One artist I know bemoaned the advent of the computer in the art department; she likes the smell of markers).

2. Changes in client fee structures – This may be a case where the computer is just too efficient for its own good. If your agency charges clients an hourly fee for creative services, the agency will in effect be losing money since the computer is faster with some tasks, and therefore the agency accumulates less billable hours. Thus you may want to increase your hourly fee. Of course, such cost savings may encourage the advertiser to have the agency produce more work.

3. Changes in pricing – Many agencies still charge their clients a surcharge for all outside services and supplies. Since computers eliminate the need for traditional outside typesetting and a large number of stats, this fee will be cut back drastically. On the other hand with the power of the computer, you can accomplish new tasks, like stripping, spot color separation, and 4/color builds, which used to be the sole domain of the printer and the color separator.

4. Changes in time schedules – The speed of the computer is one of its significant attributes. Yet, the faster you can complete work the faster account executives and clients will expect it done. This will be reflected in an increased workload. It's a vicious cycle.

5. The need for trained personnel – Despite how user-friendly computers have become, it still takes three to six solid months of working with the computer to become highly proficient. For that reason qualified graphic artists are few and in great demand. They will command more pay and are more difficult to replace.

For as many problems as the computer will solve for the art director, it also presents an equal number of problems and challenges. In this chapter, I have only scratched the surface of what the computer can do. It will take time, experimentation and creativity on your part to take advantage of the depth of the graphic computer's enormous powers.

CHAPTER VIII

Miscellaneous Matters

There are a number of different aspects of advertising that don't come under any specific heading, but are worth exploring.

Art Direction and the Law

The Campbell Soup Story – Condensed Version

They were finally ready for the soup. The photographer made his final exposure adjustments. The prop stylist had just set the table. The assistants were anxiously waiting to take the film for processing and to break down the set for the next shot.

In the far corner, you could hear the whirling of a can opener as the familiar red, white and gold can was spinning. The food stylist was just about to pour its contents into the bowl, a rather plain looking piece of dish ware except for the bed of glass marbles in the bottom.

So the stage was set for one of the most well-known cases of deception in advertising history. The case involved the Campbell Soup Company, and an advertisement. Because of the marbles in the bowl, the vegetables in the soup stood out, implying the soup was chock full of those ingredients. The courts ruled it a case of deceptive product advertising. Campbell Soup withdrew the ad and now depicts its products very carefully.

Whether Campbell's tried to deceive their customers is not the question for us. But try to imagine, if you can, that you were the art director on the shoot. Imagine all those vegetables going to the bottom of the plate, as vegetables are prone to do. Pretend this was just the first shot in many shots that had to be accomplished that day. What would you have done? You might have asked yourself, "What harm would it do? After all, the vegetables are in there even though they don't want to cooperate for the camera."

This is just one of hundreds of cases that illustrate the need for art directors to be aware of the law and how it affects advertising. Even if an advertising agency has the benefit of a lawyer on staff, that won't necessarily prevent agencies from getting into legal entanglements.

Forewarned is forearmed. Whether you know it or not, as an art director you're constantly brushing with the law. That's why it's extremely important to develop an understanding of law and how it affects your job. The chance of being involved in a case of deception may seem remote, but it is not impossible.

In this section we'll examine a number of legal issues in advertising as they affect art directors. We will try to get some sense of the legal boundaries and how you can avoid crossing them.

Deception. Naturally, every advertiser wants to put his or her best foot forward, and show their product in the best possible light. But as Dean Keith Fueroghue, head of his own agency and a former art director himself, points out in his book, <u>But the People in Legal Said...</u>,"When the strengths [of a product or service] are distorted, or when significant weaknesses are are either played down or ignored altogether, a deception is created."* Some deceptions may be subtle, such as with Campbell Soup. Other times, an advertisement can be blatantly fraudulent – that is, out and out lying about a product. For instance:

L'Aiglon Apparel, a women's clothing

* "But the People in Legal Said...", Dean Keith Fueroghue, Dow Jones Irwin,

manufacturer, created an ad campaign selling a ladies' distinctively designed dress for $17.95, which was sold through the mail. In the ad the dress was photographically depicted along with the price. This ad ran for some time and became strongly associated in the public's mind with L'Aiglon.

The story continues how Lana Lobel, a retailer, sold a clearly different dress of much lower quality – also available through mail order, at the price of $6.95. Yet, Lobel used the exact photo of the L'Aiglon dress in their own ad. The purpose was to deceive the public into thinking that the L'Aiglon and the Lobel dress were one and the same.

By far the greatest number of deception cases involve comparative, or head-to-head advertising. In comparative advertising one advertiser will pit its product against a competitor or the industry at large. An example of this is the famous "Where's the beef?" TV commercial for Wendy's fast food restaurants:

The commercial opens on three elderly woman at a fictional fast food restaurant, with signs in the background declaring the "home of the fluffy bun." The commercial made an over night star of octogenarian, Clara Pellar, who boldly declared, "Where's the beef?" after being served an enormous bun, *sans* meat. No one specific competitor of Wendy's was named although everybody understood the commercial was aimed at the other fast food giants – McDonalds, Burger King, et al. This form of competitive advertising is very general in its claims and therefore non-damaging.

Other comparative advertising can become quite specific, using actual brand names, trademarks, and packaging or image ads and commercials. There is nothing illegal about this unless a deception is created.

Quality Pure, a shampoo manufacture was unsuccessful when they made the comparison between their baby shampoo and Johnson & Johnson's Baby Shampoo. Quality Pure manufactured a line of baby products whose packaging bore a striking resemblance to J&J's product. At a glance it would be easy to confuse the two.

Quality Pure ran a 30 second commercial that compared their product to Johnson & Johnson's. In the spot spokesperson, Jane Pauley, stated that the Quality Pure brand gave her "the same lather" as Johnson & Johnson's Baby Shampoo. The commercial went on to make further claims that the quality and results were exactly the same from both brands.

Consequently, Johnson and Johnson brought suit against Quality Pure. The court ruled that advertising on basis of price was perfectly acceptable. But it was totally unacceptable to "sell a competing product on the basis of a lower price and at the same time use [packaging] designed and calculated to fool the customer into the belief that he is getting someone else's product."

An ad doesn't even have to be blatantly deceiving to be misleading. It can be deceptive even if it has only a tendency to deceive.

Several years ago Jacobsen (a division of Textron) ran an ad campaign directed to dealers, comparing the virtues of its Sno-Burst snow thrower and the Toro Snow Master. The campaign touted the slogan, "The New Jacobsen. You Get More To Sell." The advertising drew a comparison between the two brands using the criteria of reserve power, engine size, starter priming, gas/oil ratio, wheel size, snow-throwing distance, fuel capacity, auger housing, handle adjustment, and warranty.

As you would expect, the Jacobsen outscored the Toro in all categories. Toro brought suit against the parent company, Textron. The court ruled that even though the claims made by Jacobsen were true, the differences were insignificant and arbitrary. For instance, Jacobsen claimed the Toro needed priming before it would start. But starting the Jacobsen also required pulling the starter cord several times which the court said was also priming. Thus the comparison was rendered false.

Other claims were true but insignificant. As an example, Jacobsen stated their handle was adjustable, which is true but only by an inch and not the basis for a just comparison, and thus misleading. Toro couldn't show a undeniable deception but it did make a strong case that Jacobsen's advertising tended to deceive.

The penalty for deceptive advertising is normally an order to desist running the misleading ads. The offending company may even be required to run corrective advertising to offset the effect of the deceptive ad. And finally, if a company can show loss of sales owing to deceptive advertising, the company can even claim monetary damages.

As part of a larger case involving a flagrant disregard for laws governing deception, Ryder, a truck rental company ran ads using false results from consumer surveys and at the same time advertised special rates, leading the public to believe those were Ryder's standard rental rates. The main theme throughout the advertising was that Ryder, a Jartran company, had superior service at a much better price than U-Haul. It was noted in the course of the proceedings that in some of the advertising, where Ryder trucks were photographed side by side with U-Haul trucks, the U-Haul trucks were positioned to appear absurdly smaller than their actual size and less attractive. Ryder lost the case on a number of counts and had to pay U-Haul, thus becoming one of the first companies to pay monetary damages due to deceptive advertising.

Right to privacy. The right to privacy, protects a person from having their image or persona used without his or her knowledge or permission for the profit of others.

A recent and celebrated case involved Christian Dior, a company that is extremely sensitive regarding the illegal use of its own name and trademark, which was itself on trial for illegally using the image of a popular celebrity.

In the early 1980's Dior ran a series of ads featuring a fictitious Dior family. The ads depicted "the Diors," the epitome of the jet-setting, idle rich in a variety of family gatherings, including the marriage of two Diors, the birth of a baby, and their ascent to heaven.

The famous court case concerned the ad illustrating the marriage of the Diors. The exclusive gathering of friends of the couple included the likes of movie critic Gene Shalit, model Shari Belfonte Harper, and actress Ruth Gordon, as well as Barbara Reynolds, a real life secretary who bore an uncanny resemblance to Jackie Onassis.

The advertiser knew from reputation that Ms. Onassis would never allow her person to be used to promote any commercial product. In light of this they approached Ron Smith Celebrity Look-Alikes, to provide an Onassis double. What the Dior company didn't know was that even the use of a look-alike requires the permission of the celebrity when the look-alike is impersonating the genuine article.

I have highlighted these particular cases because at some point an art director was involved. Whether it was designing the ad, developing a concept, directing a photo shoot or television commercial, at some point an AD had the opportunity for input – to suggest some caution and prudence, by recommending legal advice. Allowing your agency to fall into a legal bind could not only cost the agency money, it could also put you out of a job. If you have any question as to the legality of any advertisement, talk to your agency's legal department, or consult your agency's lawyer.

Contracts. Every day, whether you realize it or not, you are entering into contracts. Whenever you hire a photographer, every time the typesetter picks up a job, any time you fill out a purchase order for art supplies, you are entering into a contract.

A contract, as defined by Tad Crawford in his book, "Legal Guide for the Visual Artist", states: A contract is an agreement creating legally enforceable obligations between two or more parties.*

While the terms of most contracts are simple – an art store agrees to deliver supplies in new condition in exchange for prompt payment of bills – making a contract with other suppliers, especially photographers and illustrators, is much more involved, with questions of copyrights, reproduction rights, and other rights to be negotiated.

The object of the contract is not to "put one over" on the other party. Rather a fair contract assures that both parties will benefit from the agreement. Verbal contracts are as legally binding as written contracts, although it's preferable to work from written contracts to avoid any misunderstanding as to the specifics of the contract.

When forming a contract, consider what benefits, and terms are important to you, your agency, and your client. How about copyright ownership, and reproduction rights? (We will be discussing these in greater depth later in this

---

* Legal Guide for the Visual Artist, Tad Crawford, Allworth Press, 1989

chapter). How about delivery dates? Will you need a preliminary sketch before the final illustration is completed? And payment – how much, in what increments, and when will the balance be due? These points are all open for negotiation, and should be included in your agreement.

I've included my standard agency contract for photography, on Page 118, as an example. Modify it or create your own, *but be sure you have your agency lawyer review any legal contract that you intend to use.*

Copyright

In 1790 the Congress of the United States passed the Copyright Act, the purpose of which was, "To promote the Progress of Science and useful Arts, by securing for limited Times to Authors the exclusive Right to their...Writings...." Over the years the interpretation of "authors" has been broadened to include not only writers, but painters, sculptors, illustrators, film makers, recording artists, and photographers as well.

Under copyright law, a work of art is protected against duplication without the permission and compensation to the artist. In addition, the artist has the right to specify the number of times the work is to be reproduced and the specific media where it is to appear.

For instance, if you commissioned an illustration for an advertisement in a magazine, and at a later date you decided to use the same art for a billboard, you would have to obtain the artist's permission and probably pay further compensation to the artist, unless he or she has given up the copyright.

What is copyrightable? A work is applicable for copyright if it meets the criteria of being both *original* and *creative*. By original, it's meant that the work can't be a copy of another work, even if it's done in another medium. For instance, the movie <u>Gone With the Wind</u>, is based on the book by Margaret Mitchell, thus the movie storyline is not eligible for copyright (although the movie as an interpretation of the book is copyright worthy).

Agency Photography Contract

This is to confirm that_____(Agency) on behalf of_____.
(Client) has entered into contract with_____(Photographer) to provide photography under the agree upon terms below:

Agency is the lawful representative of the Client.

The Photographer will provide photography that meets the objectives agreed upon between the Agency, Client and the Photographer

The Photographer agrees that the Agency and the Client are not responsible for acts of nature, that might delay shooting on location outdoors and will not be charged in such an event

The Agency and the Client agree to permit the Photographer use of the photography for reproduction for printed promotional pieces or for awards competition

The price agreed to in this contract is firm and all inclusive

The Client will retain ownership of copyrights to the photography

The Client will retain all reproduction rights

The Client will retain all ownership rights to the original photography, whether negatives, transparencies or prints

The Photographer is responsible for providing quality in photography reflective of current standards in the industry (sharpness, contrast, color fidelity, etc.)

The Photographer takes full responsibility for the work performed by suppliers (i.e. photo labs, model makers, models, stylists, food stylists), in their hire

If the Photographer fails to produce satisfactory photography, he/she will be responsible for the expense of all outside suppliers involved in the photosession

The Photographer and his or her employees are responsible for conducting themselves properly when working with the Agency's Clients and Client personnel

The Photographer agrees to photograph the shot as portrayed in the layout with enough bleed for reproduction unless otherwise directed by the Agency

The Photographer is responsible for delivering the transparencies or negatives within 48 hours of the photosession unless otherwise agreed upon

The Agency will pay ⅛ of the Photographer's day rate (for an 8 hour day) for overtime over an 8 hour day, up to the twelfth hour

The Photographer will be responsible to bring all necessary materials, equipment, proper supplies of film to do his or her job properly

The Agency agrees to pay the Photographer the amount below upon delivery and acceptance of the photography

Contract Price $_____

Photographer's Signature_____ Date_____

Agency Representative's Signature_____Date_____

Creative means that the work is artistic or possesses at least a minimal sense of esthetics. Furthermore, to be copyrighted, a work must be in a fixed form of expression. A performance isn't copyrightable, but a video recording of that performance, which is a fixed image on tape, can obtain a copyright.

An idea is not eligible for copyright. An idea for a story about a New England town that is being terrorized by a 25 foot shark is not copyrightable, but the specific story, "Jaws," by Peter Benchley is.

New Copyright Law. In 1978 the new copyright law went into effect. Some of the features of the new law include an extended term of copyright, lasting for the life of the artist, plus fifty years, (the previous was 28 years, plus a renewal for another 28), and broadening the types of copyrightable art forms, with the ability to terminate the transfer of copyright after a specified time.

Work-for-hire. The most significant revision of the copyright law for art directors is the work-for-hire provision. Under the new law, a work-for-hire situation entitles the employer or commissioning party to ownership of the copyright. Where the problem lies, though, is determining what constitutes a work-for-hire situation.

The Graphic Artists Guild and the American Society of Magazine Photographers, two well organized and powerful lobbying groups, would like to have the work-for-hire clause restricted to those employees working 9 to 5, Monday through Friday, and receiving full employee benefits. Any other artist who does not conform to this definition, they deem a freelancer and thus entitled to the copyright ownership of all work. The Supreme Court, in fact, upheld their position in a ruling during the 1989 session.

So, even if you've paid an artist fairly for his or her work, you have not hired that person and are obligated to pay continually for the repeated right to use the work.

I feel, it's in the client's best interest to obtain the copyright (what is termed a buy-out), or rights to unlimited usage for all work. For the extra fee involved, it pays to have the freedom to use a piece of work whenever and wherever you choose.

Copyrighting the client's ads. At the same time you want to make sure to copyright all material that the agency produces on behalf of your client. While it's true all work produced is, under law, automatically copyrighted upon completion, it's to your advantage to go about the proper procedure of placing copyright notification on the work, and to formally register the work with the Copyright Office of the United States.

The proper notification of copyright should appear on all art, brochures, advertisements, etc. as follows: **1.** The prefix ©, or Copyright, or Copr. **2.** the year of publication or the year of creation and **3.** the name of the artist or the holder of the copyright, which may be your client.

Example: Copyright 1991 Widgets International, Inc.

For further details and information on the subject pick up a copy of <u>Legal Guide for the Visual Artist</u>, by Tad Crawford. This complete, well written and easily understandable volume on copyright and other legal concerns is a good investment. If you would like free copyright information or an application form, you can write the Copyright Office, Library of Congress, Washington, D.C. 20559, or call (202)287-9100.

Moral Rights. Artist's groups are now pushing for legislation that would entitle artists to, what has been termed, *moral rights*. Under this new proposal, an artist has the right to determine how their work is to be displayed, even if they have already sold the copyright to another party. The idea behind this law is that a work of art is representative of an artist's abilities, and that any distortion of that work is a misrepresentation of the artist abilities and possibly may be detrimental to the artist's reputation.

What does this mean to you as an art director? Let's say, for instance, you have commissioned an illustration, but because the client added more copy, you have to crop a portion of the work. The artist has the right to prevent cropping of a work for reproduction that the artist deems unnecessary or destructive to the integrity of the artwork.

Another example: you hire a photographer, who in shooting inadvertently cuts off a part of the subject. The art director must obtain the permission from the photographer before engaging an air brush artist to correct the photographer's work.

Art directors would be at a great disadvantage if they had to get permission from artists to do what's expected of them in serving their clients.

The concept of moral rights is commonplace in different European countries, and lobbying groups in our own country are already hard at work to have such national legislation become law. What the repercussions are of such a law will be interesting to see.

Television

Because television is such a highly visual medium, it's not unusual for the art director to be in charge of producing TV commercials. However, since the average cost of producing a national commercial ranges from $20,000 to $150,000 it's not a responsibility to be taken lightly. There's no substitute for careful planning to ensure the successful production of a TV commercial or video.

Movie director Alfred Hitchcock was known as the master of suspense, but to those in the movie industry he was also the master of careful planning. Hitchcock felt that the creative process should take place long before cameras ever began to roll. That is obvious when you study his most memorable and complex camera shots; these are not the result of spur of the moment inspiration.

Careful planning will yield the best results at the least cost. Costuming, casting, sets, props, location, camera angles, lighting, music, special effects, etc.; these are considerations which ought to be settled well before ever setting foot on the set.

It all starts with the story board. For the purposes of quoting the TV production, the story board should include enough visual information to get an accurate quote from your production house. The story board should account for changes of scenes and location. The camera angles should be indicated by your drawings. All significant cuts from one scene to the next should likewise be depicted. If you plan to superimpose type, or you intend to create special effects this should also be indicated. The number of actors, their style of dress, etc. – all this will figure into getting a realistic quote.

If you ever need an example of an effective storyboard, go to the local drug store and pick up a Batman or Superman comic. The appeal of action comics for kids is the ability to tell a story with the greatest economy of words, and the liberal use of pictures to move the story forward. TV is an action medium. The story board should convey a sense of action very much like a comic book. A great resource for creating effective story boards is the book, <u>Drawing Comics the Marvel Way</u>, by Stan Lee (of Spiderman fame) and Tom Buscema.

Choosing the right production house. There are two types of television production houses. First, there's what I would call the **production facility**, a company which owns its own facility and equipment, and has directors and producers on staff.

Then there's the **production company**, which promotes itself as more of a creative service, comprised of directors and producers, owning no equipment, rather renting equipment and hiring the necessary camera crew when needed. From my experience, the costs of producing a commercial with either are generally within a close range. The advantage of having all equipment and staff under one roof is convenience. On the other hand, working with a particular director or producer may override other decisions.

Begin by collecting sample tapes ("reels") from the various production companies and facilities. This library of tapes will be your resource in determining which production house to use. The details involved in producing a commercial are so great that it pays to let the production house handle as many of the details as you feel comfortable delegating, or the budget will allow. Besides organizing the crew and cameras, look to the professionals to hire composers for original music, gathering on-camera talent and announcers, reviewing tapes for voice-over announcers, scouting locations for shooting, building sets, arranging for makeup artists, prop and food stylists, etc.

Your responsibility will be to put your final OK on the selection of talent, design of sets, shooting locations, and so on. It will also be your duty to provide product packaging when needed, and producing art cards, copy cards, and photography when called for.

Who's who in TV commercial production. At various stages of the production, you will have direct contact with three different members of the production staff: the director, the producer, and the editor.

The director. This is the person you'll be working with most closely throughout the production. The job of the director is much more involved than sitting in the director's chair barking out commands to actors and crew. From beginning to end, the director is involved in all aspects of the production. During pre-production you'll work with the director reviewing the storyboard, interviewing talent, deciding on set design and location shooting, selecting props, reaching agreement on format (film vs. video tape) and other artistic aspects of production.

On the set, the director oversees the cast and crew. The director is the commander, approving lighting and final set construction. The director will give his or her seal to the camera angle, and camera moves, as well as directing the actors.

Finally, the director will see the commercial through the editing stage. The director will review the footage and – based on your story board and script – select the best takes, instruct the editor where to make the cuts, where exactly to incorporate special effects, where to bring in the background music and the voice over announcer.

The success of your commercial depends in no small

part on the calibre of the director. Selecting the right director will bring out the best in your commercial, so choose wisely.

The producer. Consider this person as the facilitator. He or she is the person behind the scenes, working to assist the director and coordinating the various elements of production. Where the director is responsible for the artistic side of the production, the producer is the nuts and bolts individual – the detail person – scheduling studio and editing time, hiring crew, arranging for equipment, negotiating production costs, even handling details such as catering for meals. And if there are any snags or problems with the final product, the producer will be the person you'll be dealing with to rectify the situation.

The producer will pave the way for everyone else to do their job in an efficient and timely fashion.

The editor. The editor is the last person involved with the commercial production, and there can be no underestimating the importance of his or her contribution. Today's editor is a technician whose tools are a wide variety of electronic instruments, including the switcher used for making cuts, dissolves and wipes from scene to scene; the chiron or type generator; audio equipment, and numerous special effects machines. Just as an artist's pencil and markers are an extension of his artistic expression, the competent editor must be facile in manipulating these various pieces of editing equipment.

The pre-production meeting. I can't stress strongly enough the importance of holding a pre-production meeting. Once all of the details have been worked out and the final production costs confirmed, schedule the client, the account executive, and the director and producer to meet and review the upcoming production. This will help ensure no details have been overlooked, and that there will be no surprises once the client sees the finished spot. The pre-production meeting is also the ideal time to make final suggestions or changes to the script. Furthermore, I would recommend recapping the meeting in a memo to be distributed to all parties concerned.

"Lights. Camera. Action." Once you're on the set, the production is pretty much in the hands of the director. No one will keep you from making suggestions, but realize that the slightest change could involve the cast, lighting people, sound technicians, camera men, grips, and other crew members – and that means higher costs.

Considering some productions, changing a camera angle can literally cost you thousands of dollars. That's why it's important to resolve all production problems and details well before expending studio time.

Your role on the set is to oversee the production – to make certain that the story board is being adhered to. As the crew begins to set the lighting and camera angle – before everything's in place – this should be the time you are observing and giving your input.

Furthermore, before a shot can be determined complete, you must give your OK, certain that you have the footage you need in the can, that none of the actors flubbed their lines, that the product is displayed prominently, that boom microphones weren't accidently filmed in the scene, etc. Today, that approval process is much easier with video tape, in that you can replay the results of the scene immediately after shooting. In fact, even when shooting in film, it's not uncommon to have a secondary video camera along side the film camera for this very purpose.

Be certain you have exactly the footage you need, because going back later to shoot additional footage will be very expensive.

"Cut. Print. Now let's go edit." Most editing for TV commercials today is done on video tape in a video editing suite. Even commercials shot on film are transferred to video tape, since the final product will be a video cassette sent to the TV stations. Besides, video tape is much easier to edit and incorporating special effects is much simpler on video tape than film.

The act of editing a TV commercial is a long and tedious process. What with slicing, special effects, adding the music bed, incorporating a voice-over announcer, making dubs can take as long as the actually shooting the commercial footage.

Putting a commercial together takes considerable forethought, and that's the value of having an experienced editor.

A matter of style. Over the last several years we've seen a number of different styles in TV commercials. MTV videos popularized a frantic, fast cutting style. And with the progress made in computer animation, we have seen a whole generation of special effects become commonplace. Even black and white commercials have resurfaced and have been used to great advantage.

I would caution, though, not to let fashion dictate substance. The style of the commercial should work to communicate the benefits of the client's product or service, and should not be an end in itself. Even though they're as old as the hills, the standard head shot, slice-of-life, and straight forward product demonstrations are still plenty effective for many products.

Bone up. Video and film production is a world unto itself. Now that you have a brief overview of this medium, I would recommend you do further studying on the subject. Read what you can on basic production techniques. Become acquainted with the technical side of the process. Learn the language of film and video. Most of all, study TV commercials. Determine what works, what doesn't, and why.

Working With Suppliers

"Hey, Joe," the pressman called as the supervisor came walking by, "I don't understand this." The two examined the printed piece just as the presses began to roll. They decided to call the salesman on the account, who, in turn, informed the agency. It seems a headline on the front of the leaflet had two words transposed making the message confusing. The problem was rectified and what could have been a disaster on a run of 150,000 pieces turned out to be just a negative change and re-plating by the printer. So, ends my own true life lesson on the importance of using good suppliers.

Your success as an art director will in no small way depend on the quality of your suppliers. Those suppliers might include: typographers, separators, retouchers, stat houses, printers, and photo labs. Photographers and illustrators can also be considered suppliers. Building a strong, healthy relationship with those outside services will prove its worth again and again.

Every supplier will have certain merits and shortcomings. The appropriateness of one supplier over another will depend on a number of factors – cost, quality, speed of delivery, experience and ability.

I would recommend cultivating a group of proven suppliers. Limiting your number of suppliers and using them consistently. This will benefit you in several ways:

1. Being able to negotiate lower prices

2. Having suppliers learn your likes and dislikes, which should ensure you getting the results you want

3. Persuading the supplier to expedite your work when you're faced with a time crunch

4. Enlisting the supplier's help in eradicating cost overruns

5. Encouraging the supplier to give all your work special attention

6. Relying on the supplier to alert you if problems are anticipated with a job

The art director/supplier relationship. All lasting relationships are built on trust and mutual respect. If a supplier feels you're always trying to beat down the price, if your first reaction is to blame the supplier for mistakes, if every job you give the supplier needs to be done at a breakneck pace, then the relationship is doomed to fail.

Any good business relationship is based on give and take. If a supplier performs exceptionally well on an assignment, be quick to applaud the effort. If problems with a job arise, be willing to sit down and discuss the matter.

In no way am I advocating that you shouldn't be demanding. If a job is delivered and doesn't measure up to your levels of quality, I wouldn't accept it. On the other hand, there's nothing to be gained by being hard-nosed. If a mistake is made, decide for yourself – does it destroy the integrity of the piece, has the quality of the piece been sacrificed, or is the result just slightly different than what you anticipated?

If you are dissatisfied with the work or the service from an outside provider, let the provider know of your dissatisfaction. Then, take steps to ensure a similar situation doesn't crop up in the future.

Foolproof method of getting better work from suppliers. One way I've found to get better results from suppliers is to have pre-production meetings. We've already discussed pre-production meetings with photographers and TV production houses. Well, the same holds true with other suppliers, especially printers. I would suggest meeting with the printer's production people well before a job goes to press. Their production people will inform you if certain inks won't print well over another, or an effect will be hard to strip together. The production people might even offer alternate ways to achieve the same effect or a comparable, less expensive alternative.

At this stage, if there is a suspected problem with a job, it may simply mean a change on the mechanical tissue, thus avoiding costly neg changes, re-stripping, and re-plating.

In addition:

1. Whenever possible, have the supplier quote on comprehensive sketches and not on loose layouts. It's also a good practice to have the supplier re-quote a job once it's in mechanical form to make sure the initial quote is accurate and that nothing has changed on the job since the supplier first quoted.

2. Try to have several suppliers quote on a job. This will do two things.

    A. You might get a better price – which will certainly please the client. And...

    B. If you discover a great disparity in prices from several suppliers, this will give you pause to reconsider whether the project was explained properly, or whether the supplier(s) really comprehend the scope of the job

3. Keep your directions simple. Printers and separators prefer simple uncluttered mechanicals and tissues. When writing your instructions, state them in the most direct way. If you want certain headlines printed in PMS 485, color the headlines on the tissue and write next to one headline, "Print PMS 485 where indicated." If you want a photo to print as a duotone, write "Magenta and black duotone. See sample," and tape a sample duotone to the tissue. Write as little as you can, as clearly as you can. Then have your production person and the supplier rep review the boards, to see if there is any confusion.

4. Let the supplier know that you would appreciate a call, day or night, at your office or home, if they have any questions whatsoever.

It's better to miss a few minutes of <u>L.A. Law</u> to clear up confusion on a job, rather than to have the AE put you on the stand the next day, demanding to know why the job was done wrong. It wouldn't even be a bad idea to call the supplier when you know they've received the job. This will alert the supplier to review the job carefully, putting the onus on them to contact you if they foresee any problems.

Let's <u>don't</u> do lunch. You should try to preserve your impartiality when working with suppliers. As innocent as it may seem, I would refrain from letting sales reps take you to lunch or give you gifts. Ditto on personal favors no matter how friendly you are with the person or company. It may cloud your objectivity when deciding which is the best supplier to do a particular job. If the sales rep wants to give the agency a fruitcake for Christmas, I wouldn't object. That at least won't put in to question where your loyalties are when assigning a project.

It pays to be direct and above board with all your suppliers. Cover all the details and never assume anything. You've heard it said before, to assume makes an **ass** of **u** and **me.**

The Art Director and the Illustrator

While my preference is to employ photography wherever possible, well executed illustration can be used very effectively in many applications.

In newspaper advertising, for instance, illustration often reproduces better than photography. In editorial style advertising, political cartoon-like illustration is most appropriate.

For years the styles of great illustrators such as N.C. Wyeth and J.C. Leyendecker were closely associated with name brand products like Cream of Wheat cereal and Arrow Shirts, giving these products a certain amount of panache and emotion. And Norman Rockwell paintings have been a longtime source for art directors of humorous and sentimental subjects.

Illustration is also used to depict things the camera can't; i.e., anatomical drawings and architectural renderings of a building.

Types of illustration. Today the art director has an almost infinite number of illustration styles and techniques to choose from – oil and acrylics, airbrushing, watercolor, line drawing, charcoal, color pencil, scratch board – and even some new techniques using paper construction and computer-generated images.

The time it takes to execute an illustration is roughly the same as that to produce a photograph, if you take into account the amount of pre-production necessary for photography. An average illustration will take anywhere from three days to a week and a half. But remember, while the photographer can photograph several uncomplicated shots at once, the illustrator may require more time. In addition, unlike the photographer you don't have the benefit of standing over the illustrator's shoulder to assure the drawing is progressing in the right direction. Therefore, I would recommend you request the illustrator show you preliminary sketches before preceding to the finished piece.

Furthermore, give the illustrator whatever scrap (reference materials) you have on file. Provide him or her with photos of the product and any other drawings or photography you may have used in composing your layout.

Once an illustration is completed, I would have a couple of transparencies or stats taken of the final art, for two reasons: first, for your own protection in case the original should ever be lost or destroyed; second, in the case of color illustration, in particular, the illustrator often builds up an image in several layers of color. Unfortunately, the human eye perceives an illustration differently than the separator's scanner. An illustration of a plump red hot dog might look like a Havana cigar to the color scanner. With a transparency, you'll be able to detect a problem visually before you go to the expense of having a separation made.

If you plan to scan the original art, and not a transparency, request that the art work be created on a flexible surface so that it can be wrapped around the scanning drum.

While photography has great selling power, it will never eliminate the need for illustration. Luckily, today there's such a rich collection of styles, there's one to suit every purpose.

David Ogilvy's Magic Lantern

If you had joined Ogilvy & Mather in the glory days, during the late Fifties and Sixties you would have, no doubt, been ushered into a room to receive David Ogilvy's Magic Lantern, a short course on the rules of effective advertising. These are not arbitrary and dogmatic regulations, but simply a restatement of what advertising research has known for years.

You can choose to ignore these rules and label them old fashioned and inhibiting, or you can use them to your advantage to help you create more profitable advertising. Here then, is an sample of what you might have heard listening to Mr. Ogilvy:

■ Headlines with more than 10 words get less readership than short headlines. But, a study of retail advertisements found that headlines of ten words or more *sell* more merchandise than short headlines

■ When you put headlines in quotes, you increase recall by an average of 28%

■ "Before and after" photographs seem to fascinate readers. In a study of 70 campaigns with known sales results, Gallup polls did not find a single "before and after" campaign that did not increase sales

■ It has been proven that headlines set in all caps retards reading. People are accustomed to read in lower case

■ Reading headlines superimposed on photographs is difficult

■ Periods are called "full stops". You will find no full stops at the end of headlines of newspaper articles. They inhibit further reading

■ Successful magazines all use the same graphics:

1. Copy has priority over illustration.

2. The copy is set in serif type. (Sans serif type is particularly difficult to read)

3. Type is set in three columns, 35 to 45 characters wide

4. Every photograph has a caption

5. The type is set black on white, or light stock

■ Copy that starts with drop caps increase readership by 13%, all things being equal

■ If you're creating an editorial style ad and the magazine insists that you slug your ad with the word, "advertisement," set it in reverse, italics, and caps (all styles proven more difficult to read), then nobody will read it

■ Two page ads cost almost twice as much as single pages, but they seldom get twice the readership or pull twice as many coupons. Occasionally, there is a functional reason for using a double page spread, as when your product is a long one and has to be shown horizontally. However, if you swear off double spreads, you will be able to run twice as many advertisements for the same money, thereby doubling your frequency.

■ It was found that ads with photographs attracted more readers, were more believable, and better remembered

■ Don't show human faces larger than life size. They seem to repel readers

■ Advertisements in four colors cost 50% more than black and white, but on the average they are 100% more memorable

■ Readers tend to look at the illustration, then the headline, then at the body copy. So put the elements in that order, top to bottom

■ On the average, headlines below the illustration are read by 10% more people than headlines above the illustration (Amazingly, 59% of all magazine advertisements show the headline above)

■ Four times more people read the captions under illustrations than read body copy

■ If you make your ads look more like editorial pages, you will attract more readers. Roughly six times as many people read the average article as read the average ad. Very few advertisements are read by more than one reader in twenty. You can conclude that editors communicate better than ad men

■ Set key paragraphs in boldface or italic

■ Help the reader into your paragraphs with arrowheads, bullets, asterisks, and marginal marks

■ If you have a number of unrelated facts, don't use cumbersome connectives; simply number them

■ If you use spacing between paragraphs, you increase readership by an average of 12%

These rules are not intended to be followed dogmatically. At times, it will be appropriate to break the rules, but at least if you know the ground rules you can make informed decisions when you do step outside those boundaries.

Chapter IX

Advancing:
AD to CD

"So, landsmen all, wherever you may be,
If you want to climb to the top of the tree,
If your soul isn't fettered by an office stool,
Then be careful to be guided by this golden rule:
Stick close to your desk, and never go to sea,
Then you all may be the Ruler of the Queen's Navy."

Gilbert and Sullivan
from <u>HMS Pinafore</u>

I don't care who you are, everyone has some ambition to get ahead. There are two questions, though, you have to ask yourself: what does it mean to get ahead? And what are you willing to sacrifice to that end? One warning, don't be surprised if you discover that getting ahead isn't everything it's cracked up to be.

How high can you fly?

We often judge success in terms of **position.** Today the positions for advancement in the advertising industry are practically limitless. You can move up the ranks to the position of senior art director or executive art director. Beyond that, there's assistant creative director and eventually CD.

Further ahead is the title of vice president, but don't get too full of yourself. My opinion has always been that agencies breed vp's like rabbits. In 1980, Ogilvy & Mather claimed to have 324. I would be terrified to know the count today.

If you carry enough creative clout in the industry you might eventually become an agency president. And (dare I say it), there's always chairman of the board.

You may scoff, "A pipe dream." To which I would respond, "David Ogilvy, Jane Maas, Tom McElligott, Hal Riney." All creatives, who've made it to the upper, upper echelons.

With position there naturally comes the rewards of **money**. Titles are nice, but hollow if promotions aren't accompanied by an increase in pay. However, in any position there will be a top limit in earning capacity so if you want to be paid more, you must also advance. Still, don't let your pocketbook dictate your soul. Money is only one part of the equation concerning your desire to get ahead.

For many people, titles and money are meaningless if they're not in love with the work, which brings us to the last factor in your rise to the top – **job satisfaction**.

How do you measure job satisfaction? Is it the work itself? The recognition? The people you work with? The geographic area in which you work? The types of clients on the agency roster?

If what you enjoy doing and your higher ambition are in accord, more power to you. If not, no amount of money in the world will make it right.

Which way to the top?

As far as I know there are only three routes for advancing in the agency business.

1. Advancement at your present agency. If you're looking to advance, start right now right where you are. Consider your present agency. Does the company promote from within? Or do they think their own people unqualified to handle greater responsibility? Is there even room for advancement? Are the old timers so firmly entrenched, you're waiting for someone to have a heart attack?

Smart companies nurture the talent they have. They know it's more cost efficient to train and promote from within the agency than to look outside. First, the people on the inside are a known quantity; there's no guessing about their qualifications. They also know the systems and procedures of the agency, thus avoiding the standard learning curve. Finally, promoting from inside helps to build and maintain company morale. The employees know that the company appreciates their efforts and consequently they will work that much harder.

Still, even if you're working with a good agency, there may be little room for advancement. So what do you do?...

2. Move to another agency. Don't be fooled into thinking the grass is always greener at some other agency. As Erma Bombeck points out, it's also greener around the septic tank.

If you do decide to move to another agency, remember to take your time looking. Don't take the first job that comes along just to get out of your present position. Your next move should be a move with true advancement possibilities. The point is, you have a job, a steady dependable position, so stay cool and stay put.

Move cautiously. Ask plenty of questions of all prospective employers. What are their policies for advancement? Do they hold periodic evaluations? Do your homework. Who are their clients? How much have they grown in the last year? In the last five years? Talk to colleagues. What are their impressions or knowledge of the agency in question?

In time, you may get tired of working for others. Perhaps you dream of being your own boss, responsible for your own destiny, ready to blaze your own advertising trails; then it's time to...

3. Start your own agency. If you decide to start

your own agency, you can make yourself creative director, president, even emperor if you want. But until your venture gets off the ground, you'll also be the chief cook and bottle washer. I know from experience the sacrifice involved; the long hours, the low or no pay at times, the hustle of pitching new business.

Starting a business means becoming involved in business activities which ultimately keep you away from what you do best, and that's art directing. If you're absolutely determined to own your own agency, let me advise you to be the best art director imaginable, become sought after, and then buy an established agency from someone else.

Eight ways to make it to the top

Once you've settled in at an agency, here are eight specific things you can do to ensure your rise to the top:

1. Find a mentor. Find a person in the agency – the creative director, the executive art director, even a senior copywriter, and adopt them as your mentor. The dictionary describes a mentor as a wise and loyal advisor.

Your mentor will be somebody who's been at the agency for a while. He or she can be best described as professional, well respected, with a wealth of knowledge and experience. That person is someone you can learn from and emulate in many ways. They can show you how to improve your work, and when the time is right they may even recommend or sponsor you for a higher position with more responsibility.

I'm not recommending you go up to someone and announce you want him/her to be your mentor. That would be too crass. But hopefully, there's a seasoned veteran you respect, whose input and advice you regard highly. The mentorship is not an arrangement, but should be more like a relationship.

2. Be a guy or gal Friday. Always be there for your boss. If a job needs to be done, be the one who volunteers. If you know the boss is concerned with the progress of a job, stay on top of it. If experience tells you he or she likes things done a certain way, make sure things are the way the boss likes them. If there's one problem that's been plaguing your boss, fix it, if you can.

Whether you realize it or not, your boss is under added pressure and responsibility, and what he or she needs and appreciates most is someone they can depend on and who will back him or her up. If you're the person he or she comes to lean on, it should pay off at raise or promotion time.

3. Be a joiner. Join local clubs and organizations. Get your face known. Start by joining various industry groups; an advertising club, an art directors or graphics club, or the local printing/production club. But don't stop there. If you can afford the time and membership fees, join other organizations; Rotary International, local civic clubs, cultural organization, and especially your college alumni organizations.

Furthermore, don't just join...participate. There are so few people willing to donate time and effort to such groups that the person, who makes a commitment will stand out like a beacon. Eventually you will gain a reputation as the person people look to to get things done. And the positive image you build for yourself may pay off when another club member is looking for the right person at his or her agency.

4. Read. Reading is an absolute must for the forward moving AD. Magazines and books on graphics are the first and most obvious choices, but I would also encourage you to read general books on advertising. I've mentioned several throughout this book, and you'll find a more complete list in the Bibliography. Furthermore, I recommend picking up a text book or two on marketing. They're valuable reference tools, and will help to make you a more valuable well-rounded advertising person.

Self-help books are another must. One of the best is How To Win Friends and Influence People, by Dale Carnegie. Although written more than 50 years ago, How To Win Friends... is still a brisk seller, and the self help courses on which the book is based are attended by thousands of people nationwide every year. The truths put forth by Dale Carnegie are as valid today as when the book was first published. When you learn how to handle other people properly, you'll be building better personal skills, and you'll get more accomplished.

Motivational books. They're a great way to build confidence. When you read this account or that account of success, you'll begin to think to yourself if he or she can do it, I can do it. That will put you in a positive state of mind to succeed.

Subscribe to news magazines. What goes on in current affairs is often the basis of today's advertising – for instance, the Pepsi commercials that took advantage of the toppling of the Berlin Wall as a backdrop for the soft-drink's message as a taste for a "new generation."

Read entertainment magazines. Find out what's hot and who's *in* in the movies, television, the theater, and novels; they can be another source of inspiration for your ads. Fashion magazines are also a great source for current trends in color and design, as well as page layout and design of articles, stories, and other ads.

5. Think positively. Again, let me recommend Norman Vincent Peale's book, <u>The Power of Positive Imaging</u>, which describes a concept that he has espoused for years. The truth is, it works – with the right attitude almost anything is possible, including getting ahead in advertising.

People tend to gravitate to people who are upbeat. Positive people tend to be better motivators than more negative people. The positive person exudes confidence and an infectious *can-do* attitude which spreads to everyone they work with. Don't doubt it – those in a position to promote in the agency will recognize this trait.

Building a positive self image is no easy task, but I think you'll see by reading Mr. Peale's book, that it can most definitely be learned.

6. Be a good administrator. Even if you have no

one to administrate, at least be a good administrator of your own time. The person, who's looking to get ahead in advertising, has to manage others, so it's important to demonstrate any way you can that you have effective administrative ability.

7. Be imaginative. There's the story of the art director, who desired a job with Ogilvy & Mather. He decided to set up his studio in front of the O&M building, vowing to remain there until there was room upstairs at the agency for his talents. Sometimes you have to take a chance, be imaginative and do something out of the ordinary, something that will get people to stand up and take notice.

Keep your finger in the creative pie

As you gain more responsibility, the tendency is to become more administrative and less creative. Before long you realize you've traded pushing color markers for pushing papers through the agency system. In time, you're looking longingly at art directors enjoying the process of creating advertising and wondering if you even remember how to be creative.

You built your reputation and advanced in large part based on your creative talents. Don't give up what you do best, just like that.

It's important to stay on the creative front lines for two reasons: **1.** Exercising your creative side will help keep you excited and uplifted about your work, and **2.** You will be better able to judge other creative work if you maintain a familiarity with the creative process.

If it means assigning yourself a project of your own, do so. Fight the temptation of letting somebody else handle all the creative challenges.

Keep politics in Washington where it belongs

Office politics starts at the top. Even if those at the top don't encourage such action, if they let it go unchecked it will flourish. Who's being paid more; who went to lunch with whom; who was asked to make the presentation to the client; who has the biggest office – you'll spend so much time embroiled in such trivialities that your work will begin to suffer.

The politicians are always having to watch their back side to see if anybody is trying to put it to them. Whatever you do, don't get involved in office politics. Be the best art director you can, and let the Machiavellians at your agency go feasting on one another. If need be, change agencies where politics aren't an issue. In the end you'll come out on top.

On your way up
Avoid getting burned out

I think there comes a time in the life of most creative people when their life/work becomes a drudge. When every campaign seems like the one before. When the pressures of having to produce every day begins to weigh too heavily. Once you get into a creative funk such as this, it's hard to get out. You think there's no solution to the problem, and you can't see the light at the end of the tunnel.

These are the signs of advertising burnout, and if left unchecked could lead to more serious problems such as poor behavior, even drug and alcohol abuse. The question is: what to do if you find yourself beginning to burnout?

Corresponding to a feeling of burnout is a negative outlook on your work, the agency, even your personal life. If it's possible to regain the right outlook, then perhaps you can overcome burnout. But how do you change that attitude and make what you do exciting and fresh again?

1. Pursue other interests. For many ADs, art direction is an all encompassing endeavor. This can make for a very stale existence over time. If this situation applies to you, perhaps you can develop alternate interests. Take up a new hobby, or rekindle interest in an old one. If you enjoy bowling, set one night a week to go out with family and friends. If you'd like to enhance your education, take some night courses. Learn to ballroom dance. Join Toastmasters International and learn to speak in public.

Such activities will get your mind off your work and may even lend new perspectives to what you're doing on the job.

2. Make some changes in your life style. Are you in a rut at home? Are you part of the couch potato generation, frying your brain watching TV? Then, pull the plug and get out of your seat.

Start by doing something positive for yourself. If you're overweight start a diet. If you don't already have an exercise program, start one (but start slowly if you haven't exercised in a while). If you're a smoker, stop. If you drink to excess, cut back or quit. The point is, you can build a positive image of yourself when you begin to do positive, constructive things for yourself.

3. Change your work habits. Are you a workaholic? Dedication to the job is commendable, but it can be carried to excess. Make a point of leaving the office at a reasonable hour. And if you're worried you won't get all your work done during the course of the day, then reexamine your day at the office and see if there isn't wasted time during the day that could be better put to use to accomplish your work load.

Do you find yourself losing steam by mid-afternoon? Why not take a short nap at lunch. A 20 minute siesta would make a world of difference. As you might know, much of the world closes shop for a couple hours in the early afternoon. They must know something about the human psyche and physical condition that we Americans don't. They don't put the demands that we Americans put on ourselves. It's unnatural to ask the human mind and body to continue at full speed for 10 or 12 hours a day. Not only that, it's counter productive. Research has shown the most productive part of the day is the period soon after we wake.

If you work with only one copywriter in an agency that has several, maybe you need to start a new project with other creative people.

If you're overly serious at work, it might not hurt to introduce a little levity. Create a light-hearted feeling in your work place. Remember, the best creative ideas come when people are relaxed and at ease.

4. Change your dress. It's said that clothes can make the man...and the woman. You can change your mind, when you change your appearance. Why not change your dress style? Throw out those old wing tips and buy a pair of those pointy Italian shoes. Buy several fashionable dress outfits, and retire the stuffy grey dress suit. Do a make over on your mind when you make over your appearance.

5. Have problems at home? Solve them. If you're going through some tough times on the home front, try not to bring it to the office. I know that's easier said than done, but problems at home can color everything you do at work, and can contribute significantly to advertising burnout. If you're having domestic difficulties, work with your family or spouse to solve them.

6. Change jobs. Every job is going to have its pluses and minuses. But when the bad points begin to outweigh the good then perhaps it's time to look around for a new position. You may find that a new set of accounts and meeting new people is just the new lease on your creative life you were looking for.

7. Seek professional help. Large corporations recognize we all go through times of great stress, when we may need to turn to the help of a professional. These companies place no stigma on the need for professional help and actually provide counseling for their employees. They realize they've made a considerable investment in training their people and it's worth the cost to help employees when they're in need. I think the advertising industry should acknowledge the problem of burnout and take steps to deal realistically with the situation. In the meantime, find your own personal counselor or psychologist, if you're feeling burned out.

Know when to say, "enough."

Success is sometimes as much a matter of luck as ability. If you're not finding success in advertising, perhaps you should try your luck in the many other avenues for art directors, such as magazines and book publishing, package design, or art directing for a large corporate in-house advertising department. Even designing greeting cards. Every direction will have its challenges and rewards.

And in the end

Have you ever wondered how it is that a jet airplane, which is essentially tons of metal, is able to stay aloft? I am amazed every time a plane goes streaming down the runway, engines roaring, going faster and faster, when at the last second this huge body lifts off the ground and is sent speeding skyward. How is it possible? The simple fact is it's designed to fly. By it's very nature it can't help but fly.

The same applies to art directors. You've drawn, studied, and practiced to be an art director. You've trained hard to succeed. Yes, you will certainly make mistakes along the way; falter from time to time. But you'll learn from your mistakes, make mid-course corrections and once again you'll be on your way up.

What you have in this book is my experience and my thinking on the subject of success as an art director, some of which you'll take to heart, and some which won't be applicable to your situation. I hope this book will serve as a guide post along your way. You'll also learn a lesson or two on your own that you could add to this book. In that case, I'd love to hear from you. But at least, now you have the ammunition you need to forge ahead.

Art directors are special people with special talents. Most people are in awe of our *artistic* abilities, to be able to create on paper what never existed before. But just as important is the need to cultivate respect for the *director* in us.

Good luck!

Bibliography

"But the People in Legal Said...", Dean Keith Fueroghue, Dow Jones Irwin, Homewood, IL, 1989

Confessions of an Advertising Man, David Ogilvy, Atheneum, NY, 1985

Creative Management, William A. Marsteller, NTC Business Books, Lincolnwood, IL, 1988

Free Stock Photography, Infosource Business Publications, NY, 1986

How to Draw Comics the Marvel Way, Stan Lee and John Buscema, Simon and Shuster, New York, 1978

How to Make Positive Thinking Work for You, Norman Vincent Peale, Foundation for Christian Living, Pawling, NY, 1982

How to Make Your Advertising Make Money, John Caples, Prentice Hall, Englewood Cliffs, NJ, 1983

How To Win Friends & Influence People, Dale Carnegie, Pocket Books, New York, 1981

"I Can See You Naked", Ron Hoff, Andrews and McMeel, Kansas City, 1988

Legal Guide for the Visual Artist, Tad Crawford, Allworth Press, New York, 1989

Ogilvy On Advertising, David Ogilvy, Vintage Books, New York , 1985

The Personal Computer Book, Peter A McWilliams, Prelude Press, Los Angeles, 1982

Pricing & Ethical Guidelines, 6th Edition, Graphic Artists Guild, 1987

Quality Is Free, Philip Crosby, Penguin, 1985

A Technique for Producing Ideas, James Webb Young, NTC Business Books, Lincolnwood, IL, 1988

Tested Advertising Methods, John Caples, Prentice Hall, Englewood Cliffs, NJ, 1974

Write Like the Pros, Mark S. Bacon, John Wiley & Sons, New York, 1988

Index